NELSON MATHEMATICS 4

Towards Level 4

PUPILS' BOOK 2

Nelson

Thomas Nelson and Sons Ltd
Nelson House Mayfield Road
Walton-on-Thames Surrey
KT12 5PL UK

Thomas Nelson Australia
102 Dodds Street
South Melbourne
Victoria 3205
Australia

Nelson Canada
1120 Birchmount Road
Scarborough Ontario
M1K 5G4 Canada

First published by Thomas Nelson & Sons Ltd 1993

ISBN 0-17-421868-0 (single copies)
ISBN 0-17-421870-2 (pack of eight)
NPN 9 8 7 6 5 4 3 2 1

Printed in Italy

Authors and consultants
Bill Domoney
Peter Gash
Paul Harrison
Lorely James
Ann Sawyer
Diana Wright

Contributor
Paul Broadbent

Acknowledgements

Photography
Bodmin & Wenford Railway: pages 36 and 37; Colorsport: pages: 10, 79; Chris Ridgers: pages 24, 40, 48, 59, 102, 104.

Design
Julia King, Thumbnail Graphics

Illustration
Jane Cheswright
Jackie East
Peter Kent
Bethan Matthews
Kate Simpson
Helen Stanton
Stan Stevens
Nancy Sutcliffe
Taurus Graphics
Jo Wright

Produced by **Ian Foulis & Associates**

CONTENTS

The colour band at the foot of each page indicates the relevant section of the **Teacher's Resource File, Level 4.**

Addition grids

In this 3 x 3 grid the numbers are added across and down.

213	147	360	total
326	256	582	total
539	403	942	This is the total of all the four red numbers.
total	total		

Complete these grids. Only use a calculator to check your answers.

1.

128	137	
284	368	

2.

521	248	
372	416	

3.

624	139	
289	260	

4.

149	580	
263	311	

5.

125	275	
325	225	

6.

574	163	
119	286	

Make your own addition grids. Try a 4 x 4 square.

Fruit and nut problems

1. How many figs and prunes are there?
2. How many nuts are not peanuts?
3. How many black fruits are there altogether?
4. How many nuts are there altogether?
5. How many dried fruits are there altogether?

6\.

246	353	537
883	902	364
518	672	826

Use the numbers in the boxes. Write 10 different additions with answers less than 1000.

There is more about addition on page 72.

Many multiplications

25	55	75	15	35	65
29	59	79	19	39	69
22	52	72	12	32	62
20	50	70	10	30	60
26	56	76	16	36	66

Write the answers.

1. Multiply all the numbers in the blue row by 3.
2. Multiply all the yellow numbers by 6. Can you find a quick way to help you?
3. Multiply all the numbers in the '20s' column by 9. Can you find a quick way to help you?
4. Multiply all the green numbers by 10. What happens to them?
5. Double all the red numbers. What do you notice?
6. Multiply all the purple numbers by 4. Look at the last digit of each answer. What do you notice?

---

7. **Find the patterns.**

   Multiply 50 by 1, then by 2, then by 3, and so on, all the way up to 10.

   Compare your results with the 5 times table.

   What do you notice?

   50 x 1 = 50
   50 x 2 = 100
   50 x 3 = 150
   50 x 4 =

8. Now try the same with 55.

   Look for patterns.

   55 x 1 = 55
   55 x 2 = 110
   55 x 3 =

Make your own problems

Clarissa picked three cards.
They were:

4 | 3 | 6

She made all the possible multiplications she could.

They were:

43 x 6 = 258

46 x 3 = 138

36 x 4 = 144

63 x 4 = 252

64 x 3 = 192

34 x 6 = 204

She also tried:

4 x 3 x 6

3 x 4 x 6

6 x 4 x 3

6 x 3 x 4

But she found they all made 72.

Use these cards to do the same.

1. 1 | 5 | 7 **2.** 4 | 9 | 3 **3.** 8 | 0 | 6 **4.** 2 | 5 | 4

Make your own numeral cards from 0 to 9.
Put them face down.

Turn them over three at a time. Make all the possible multiplications.

There is more about multiplication on page 75.

Rounding up, rounding down

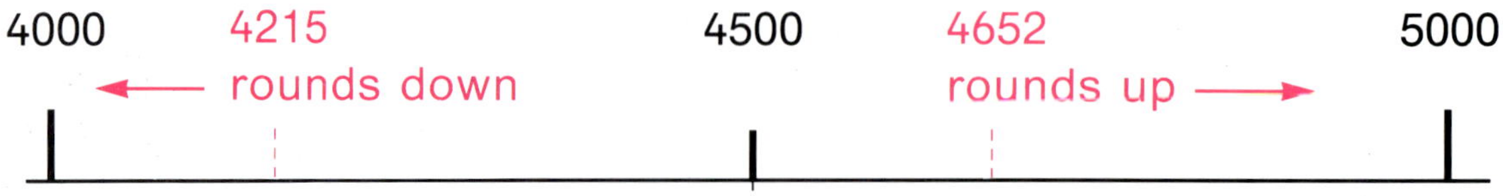

Numbers from 4001 to 4499 round down to 4000

Numbers from 4500 to 4999 round up to 5000

Round these numbers up to 5000 or down to 4000.

1. 4170	**2.** 4753	**3.** 4500	**4.** 4265
5. 4851	**6.** 4359	**7.** 4672	**8.** 4499

Here are some more 4-digit numbers. Round them up or down to the nearest thousand.

Draw a number line if it will help.

9. 2449	**10.** 6921	**11.** 8689	**12.** 3162
13. 5863	**14.** 7500	**15.** 4425	**16.** 9267

These numbers have been rounded to the nearest 1000.

What is the smallest, and largest, number they could have been?

17. 2000	**18.** 5000	**19.** 3000	**20.** 7000

Rounding money

This is a price list for a pair of curtains.

Code	Size	Current Price	Now
TX9897	46″ x 42″	£21.99	£17.99
TX9898	46″ x 45″	£25.99	£19.99
TX9899	46″ x 48″	£27.99	£20.99
TX9900	46″ x 54″	£29.99	£22.99
TX9901	46″ x 72″	£39.99	£29.99
TX9902	46″ x 90″	£49.99	£38.99
TX9903	66″ x 48″	£39.99	£29.99
TX9904	66″ x 54″	£43.99	£32.99
TX9905	66″ x 72″	£57.99	£43.99
TX9906	66″ x 90″	£69.99	£53.99
TX9907	90″ x 54″	£66.99	£51.99
TX9908	90″ x 72″	£76.99	£59.99
TX9909	90″ x 90″	£87.99	£67.99

It is helpful to round prices to the nearest pound.

For example, £21.99 rounds up to £22.

Sometimes it helps to work out costs if you round to the nearest ten pounds. For example, £22 rounds down to £20.

Round these prices to the nearest pound and nearest ten pounds.

1. £22.99 **2.** £69.99 **3.** £43.99 **4.** £39.99

5. £57.99 **6.** £25.99 **7.** £31.99 **8.** £66.99

Rounding can also help you to estimate the answer to a sum.

3192 + 5763 can be rounded to

3000 + 6000 → the answer is roughly 9000.

The true answer is 8955 which rounds to 9000.

Estimate the answers to these, then check with a calculator.

9. 3126 + 5255 **10.** 1763 + 7042

11. 4927 + 2846 **12.** 5162 + 4825

Gold, silver or bronze

Here are the points scored by competitors in different swimming events. Write the names of the people or countries who won gold, silver and bronze medals.

1.

Diving (highest score wins)	
L. Slater	108.9 points
F. Lovering	102.3 points
P. Nash	110.5 points
B. Karanov	107.5 points
F. Schultz	103.6 points

2.

100m Breast-stroke – men (shortest time wins)	
J. Warnakov	56.2 secs
D. Young	55.7 secs
P. Bermann	55.2 secs
K. Brodinski	56.9 secs
A. Holmes	58.8 secs

3.

200m Medley Relay – women (shortest time wins)	
USA	2 min 5.8 secs
CAN	2 min 6.2 secs
FRA	2 min 5.9 secs
AUS	2 min 5.6 secs
UK	2 min 6.1 secs

4.

Synchronised swimming (highest score wins)	
CAN	9.4 points
USA	8.8 points
UK	9.6 points
FRA	8.6 points
GER	9.3 points

Decimal maze

Scottie the dog wants to find his way home. He must always move to a space with a smaller number than the one he is on. He can move up, down, left or right only. His starting point is 9.8.

	9.8	9.7	7.3
8.8	9.2	9.3	8.1
7.5	4.2	9.5	4.0
6.8	4.8	4.2	6.7
5.4	5.0	3.2	4.5
4.3	5.9	2.8	

1. How many different routes can you find for Scottie to follow?
2. What is his shortest route home?
3. Make your own decimal maze for a friend to try. You could use a route moving to larger numbers only.

Decimal addition and subtraction grids

(−)

7.7	5.1	2.6
6.5	4.3	2.2
1.2	0.8	0.4

In this subtraction grid, numbers are subtracted horizontally $7.7 - 5.1 = 2.6$ and vertically

$$\begin{array}{r} 7.7 \\ -\ 6.5 \\ \hline 1.2 \\ \hline \end{array}$$

0.4 is the result of all the subtractions.

Here are some addition and subtraction grids to complete. Be careful with the signs.

1. (+)

3.6	5.1	
2.4	8.9	

2. (+)

12.2	15.7	
13.9	11.6	

3. (−)

8.3	5.4	
7.2	4.5	

4. (−)

15.6	12.3	
11.9	9.5	

5. (+)

21.4	15.8	
22.7	16.7	

6. (−)

32.6	27.8	
25.4	21.8	

7. Make up an addition and a subtraction grid of your own. Try it out on a friend. Check answers together with a calculator.

Magic squares

Remember, in a magic square each row, each column and each diagonal add up to the same number.
Fill in the missing numbers in these squares.

1.

	0.9	
1.1	0.6	0.1
		1.0

2.

		4.3
	4.2	
4.1		4.6

3.

9.4		
10.3		9.3
9.7		

4.

	24.6	
24.4	24.0	25.4

5. Make your own magic square for a friend to try.

---

6. Forgetful Frances is telling a pen pal about herself. She has forgotten to put in the decimal points. Copy the numbers and place the decimal points for her.

> Dear Clara,
> My name is Frances.
> I am 95 years old.
> I am 1368 cm tall and
> weigh 314 kg.
> My brother Tom is 60
> years old. He is 1000 cm
> tall and weighs 245 kg.

Greater or less?

Use $>$ or $<$ or $=$ to make a true statement

1. 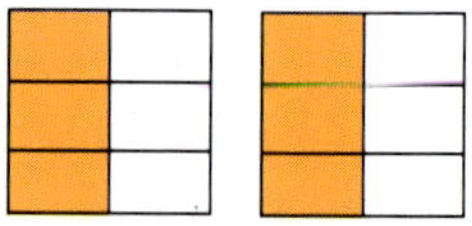

$\frac{1}{2}$ $\frac{3}{6}$

2. 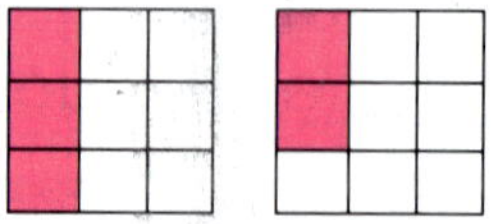

$\frac{1}{3}$ $\frac{2}{9}$

3. 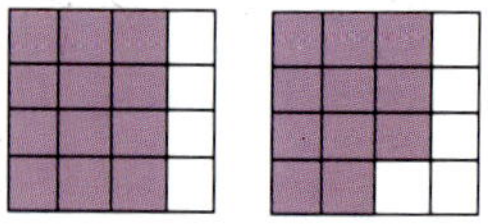

$\frac{3}{4}$ $\frac{11}{16}$

4. 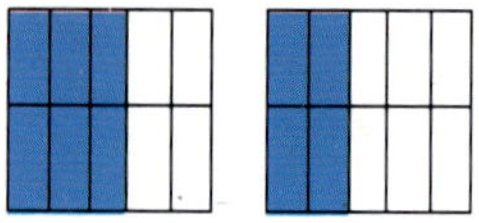

$\frac{3}{5}$ $\frac{4}{10}$

5. 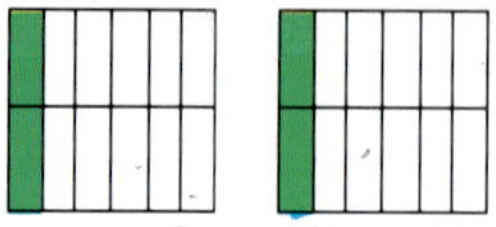

$\frac{1}{6}$ $\frac{2}{12}$

6. 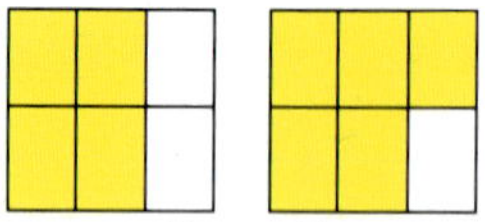

$\frac{2}{3}$ $\frac{5}{6}$

Draw pictures to help you compare these fractions.
Use $>$, $<$ or $=$ to make a true statement.

7. $\frac{1}{5}$ $\frac{3}{10}$

8. $\frac{1}{4}$ $\frac{2}{8}$

9. $\frac{5}{6}$ $\frac{9}{12}$

10. $\frac{4}{10}$ $\frac{1}{2}$

11. $\frac{2}{3}$ $\frac{5}{9}$

12. $\frac{4}{12}$ $\frac{1}{4}$

13. Two farmers have fields the same size. One plants $\frac{1}{2}$ of his with corn.

The other plants $\frac{3}{8}$ of his with corn.

Do they plant the same amount of corn?

14. Mary and Umesh have books the same length. Mary has read $\frac{3}{6}$ of hers and Umesh has read $\frac{6}{12}$ of his.

Have they read the same amount?

15. Jack and Hohy each had a mini pizza. Jack ate $\frac{5}{8}$ of his. Hohy ate $\frac{3}{4}$ of hers. Who ate more?

16. Sara may have either $\frac{1}{3}$ or $\frac{3}{9}$ of a bottle of lemonade. She likes lemonade. Which should she choose?

Put them in order

Put these fractions in order from least to greatest.
You could draw pictures to help you.

1. $\frac{1}{2}$ $\frac{3}{4}$ $\frac{3}{8}$ $\frac{5}{8}$ $\frac{1}{4}$

2. $\frac{2}{3}$ $\frac{5}{12}$ $\frac{5}{6}$ $\frac{3}{6}$ $\frac{1}{3}$

3. $\frac{4}{5}$ $\frac{3}{10}$ $\frac{2}{5}$ $\frac{1}{2}$ $\frac{7}{10}$

Put these fractions in order from greatest to least.

4. $\frac{1}{4}$ $\frac{5}{16}$ $\frac{5}{8}$ $\frac{3}{4}$ $\frac{1}{2}$

5. $\frac{7}{20}$ $\frac{3}{10}$ $\frac{1}{5}$ $\frac{3}{5}$ $\frac{9}{10}$

6. $\frac{1}{3}$ $\frac{3}{12}$ $\frac{3}{4}$ $\frac{10}{12}$ $\frac{1}{2}$

7. When you have put all the fractions in order, add another fraction to the beginning and another to the end of each set.

   Make sure they are still in order.

---

8. Make two copies of each circle. On one copy, colour 1 part of the circle. On the other, colour 2 parts. Under each circle write the fraction for the coloured part.

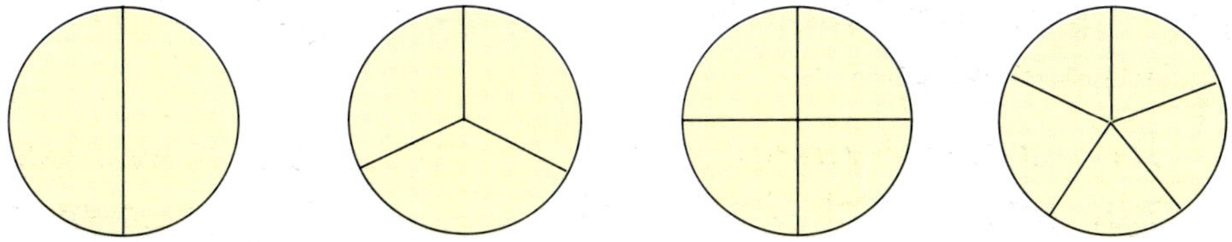

Arrange the circles in order from least to greatest, according to how much is coloured.

Decimal fractions in pictures

100 'flat'

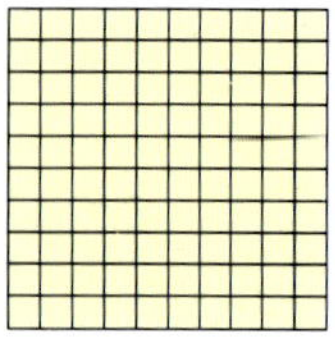

If the 100 'flat' is 1 whole one, then the 10 'long' is $\frac{1}{10}$. Written as a decimal this is 0.1

10 'long'

1 whole one
1.0

$\frac{1}{10}$
0.1

Write the decimal **and** fraction that these show.

1. 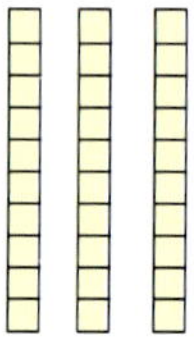

2. 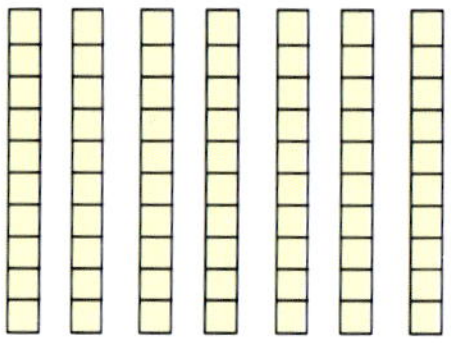

3. 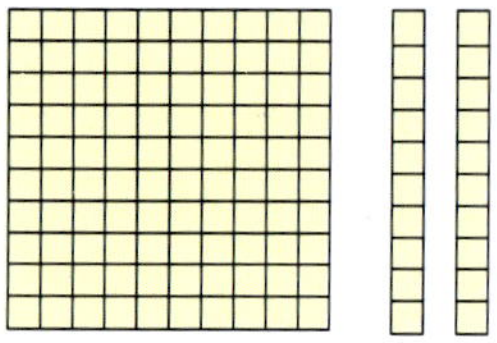

4. 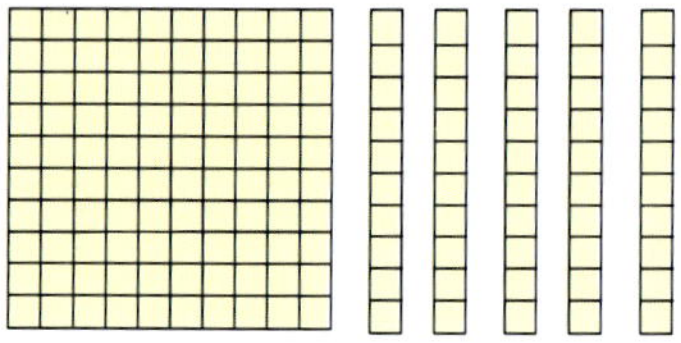

5. 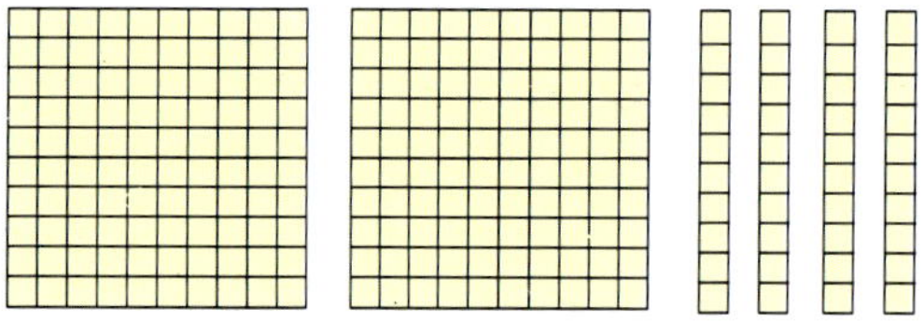

6. 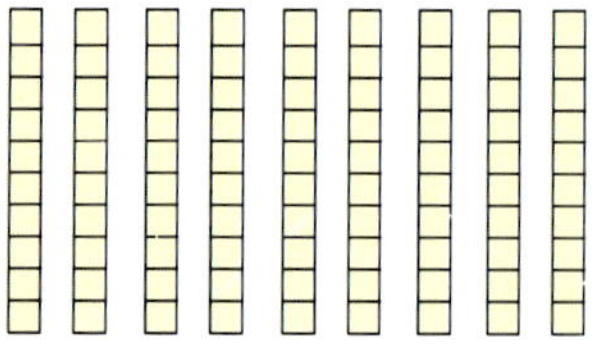

Write the decimal and fraction that these abacus pictures show.

7. 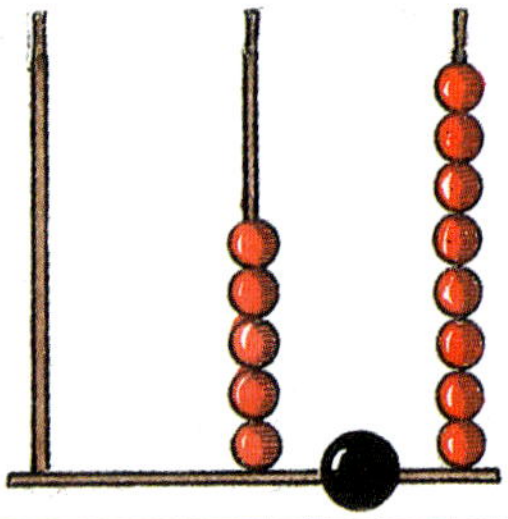

8. 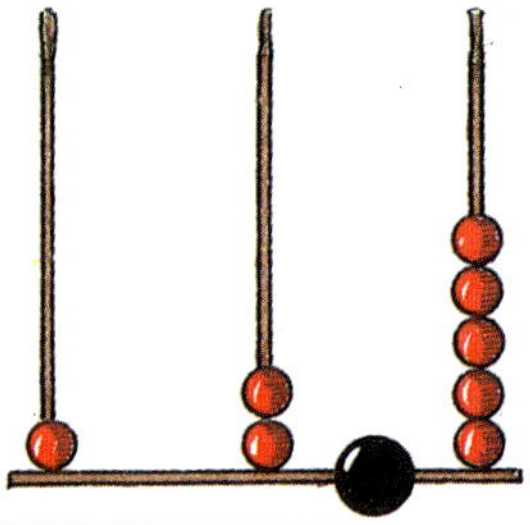

9. 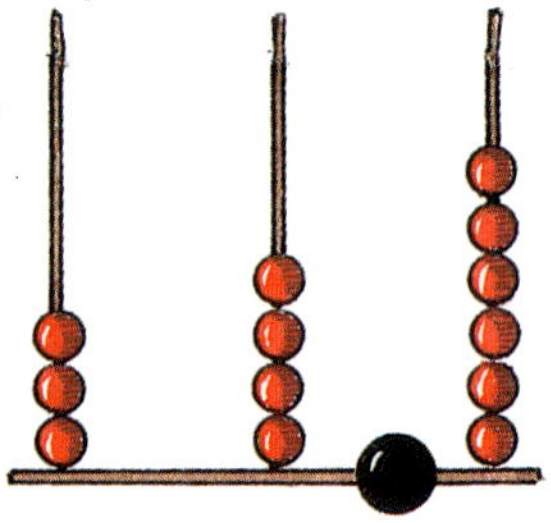

Write the decimal and fraction shown by the coloured arrows on this number line.

Other fractions as decimals

To convert a fraction to a decimal, divide the top number (numerator) by the bottom number (denominator) using a calculator.

Convert these fractions to decimals with your calculator.

1. $\frac{1}{2}$ **2.** $\frac{3}{4}$ **3.** $\frac{1}{3}$ **4.** $\frac{2}{3}$

5. $\frac{1}{5}$ **6.** $\frac{2}{5}$ **7.** $\frac{3}{5}$ **8.** $\frac{4}{5}$

9. $\frac{1}{6}$ **10.** $\frac{2}{6}$ **11.** $\frac{3}{6}$ **12.** $\frac{4}{6}$

13. $\frac{5}{6}$ **14.** Which fractions give the same decimal?

---

15. **Investigate decimal fraction patterns.**

fraction	decimal
$\frac{1}{7}$	0.1428571
$\frac{2}{7}$	0.2857142
$\frac{3}{7}$	0.4285714

Choose a 'family' of fractions like sevenths ($\frac{1}{7}$). Use a calculator to convert them to decimals.
Make a chart like this one.
Describe any patterns you see.

Good ones to try are ninths and elevenths, but try others too.

There is more about fractions on page 48.

How many ways?

All of these facts can be written about 24.

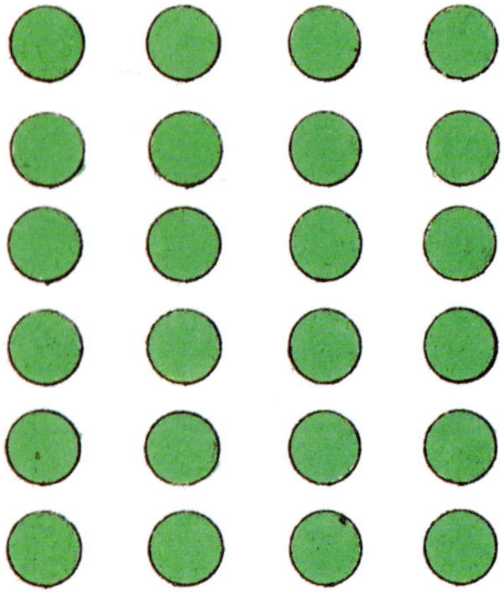

6 rows of 4 = 24

4 rows of 6 = 24

6 x 4 = 24   4 x 6 = 24

4 + 4 + 4 + 4 + 4 + 4 = 24

6 + 6 + 6 + 6 = 24

24 ÷ 4 = 6   24 ÷ 6 = 4

Do you notice that 6 x 4 makes the same as 4 x 6?

Write all the facts about these arrays.

1.

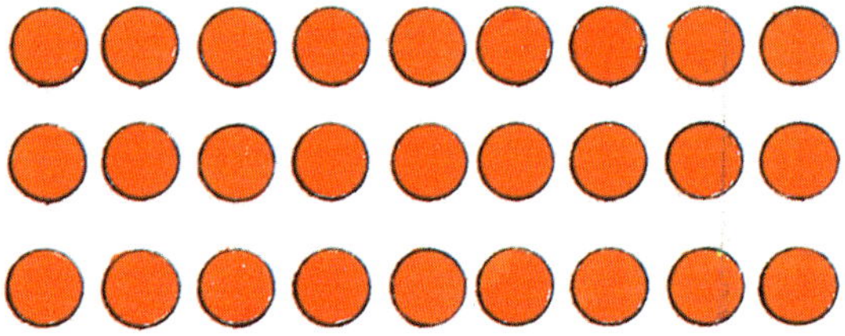

2.

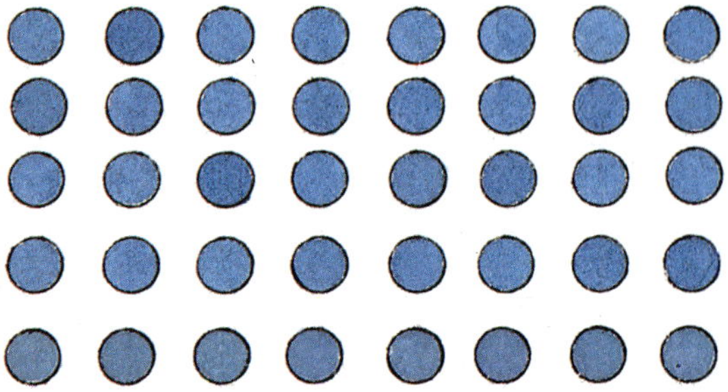

3.

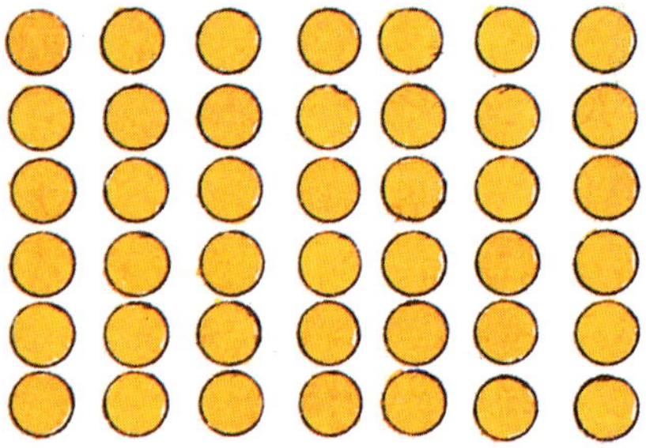

4.

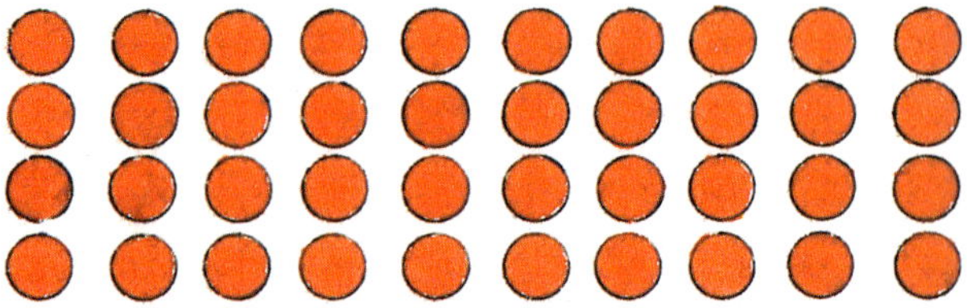

Draw these numbers as arrays and write the facts about them.

5. 32   6. 45   7. 48   8. 36

Missing operation signs

Remember: brackets make number sentences clearer.
Operations in brackets should always be worked out first.

Put in the operation signs (+, –, ÷ , x) to make these number sentences work. You may need to use brackets.

1. 2 3 4 = 1

2. 2 x 3 4 = 2

3. 2 3 4 = 3

4. 2 x 3 4 = 10

5. 8 3 x 2 = 22

6. 8 x 3 2 = 40

7. 8 x 3 2 = 12

8. 8 3 x 2 = 2

9. 8 3 x 2 = 10

10. 8 3 2 = 9

Number neighbours

A game for 2 players.

You will need digit cards from 0 to 9.

Shuffle and deal the digit cards so that each player has 5. The players lay down the digit cards in the order in which they were dealt.
To play the game, each player uses +, –, ÷ , x and = to make all the numbers from 1 to 10.
For example, here are 5 digit cards.

1 4 7 2 5

You can make 1 + 4 = 5
1 – 4 + 7 + 2 = 6

and so on.

There is more about number operations on page 50

Checking out angles

Remember: right angle  90°

acute angle 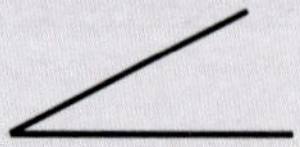 less than 90°

obtuse angle 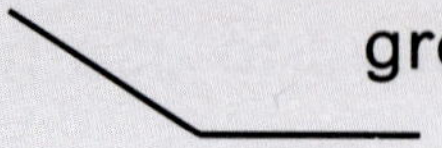 greater than 90°

Write down how many acute, obtuse and right angles these shapes contain.

1.

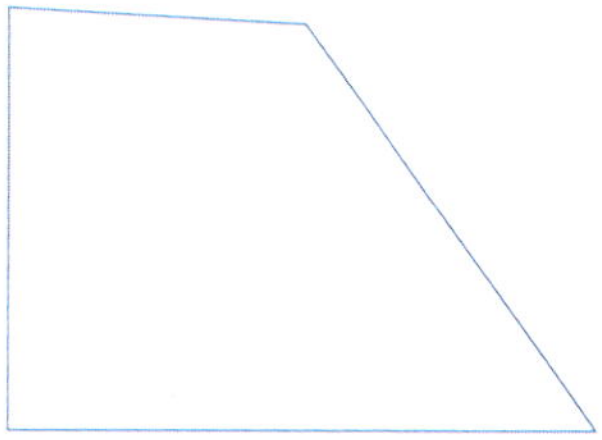

2.

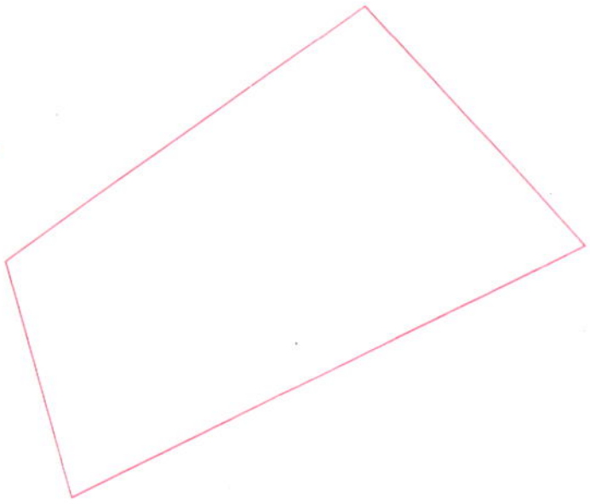

3.

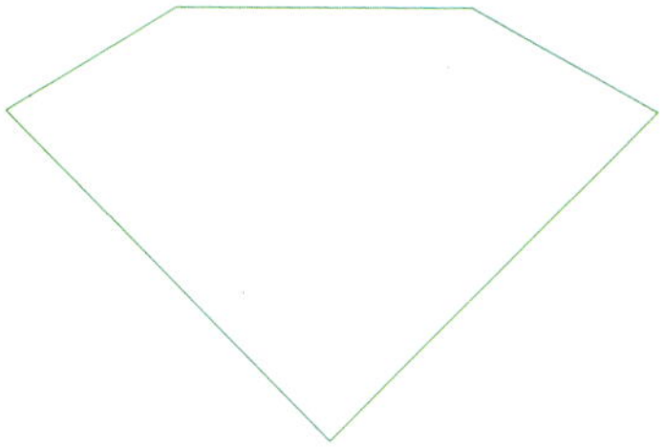

4.

5.

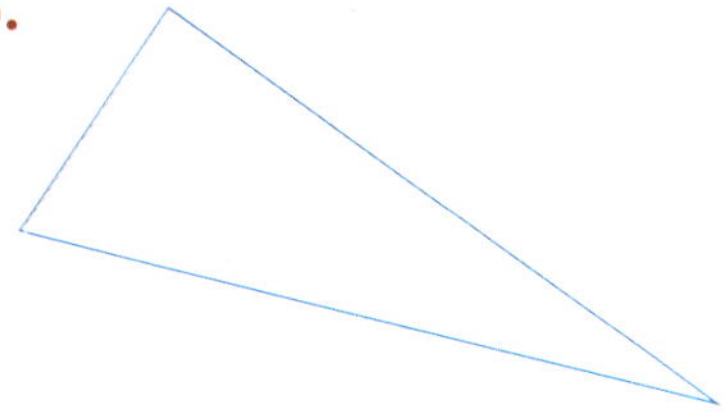

6.

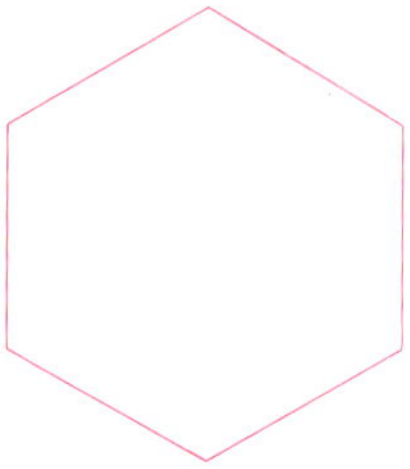

Are these angles 90°, less than 90° or more than 90°? Estimate how many degrees they are.

7.

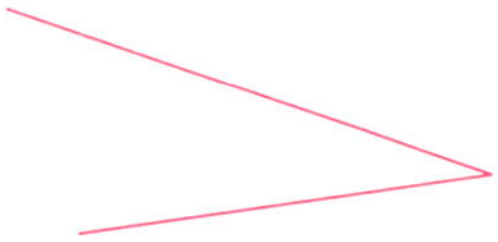

8.

9.

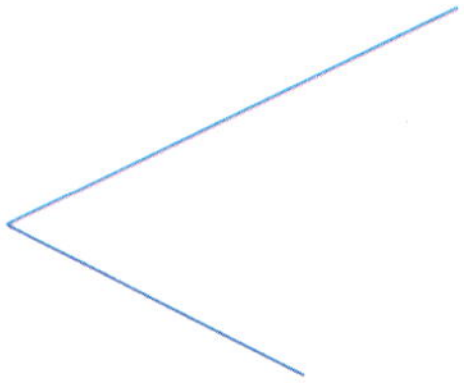

10.

11.

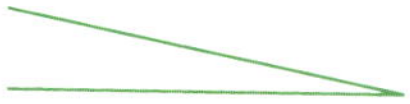

12.

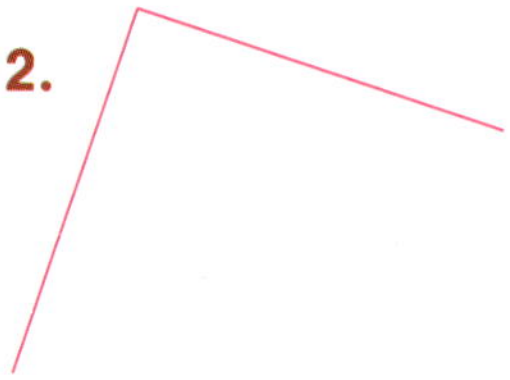

Time angles

The hands on these clockfaces make different angles, according to the times they show.

Are they acute, obtuse or right angles?

1. 

2. 

3. 

4. 

5. 

6. 

Draw clockfaces to show these times.
What sort of angles do the hands make?

7. 5:05
8. 3:30
9. 11:50
10. 9:30
11. 6:05
12. 2:40

---

13. Look for angles in the classroom.

Find 3 right angles, 3 acute angles and 3 obtuse angles.
Write them down or draw them.

Drawing circles

> You will need a pair of compasses, a ruler and a pencil.

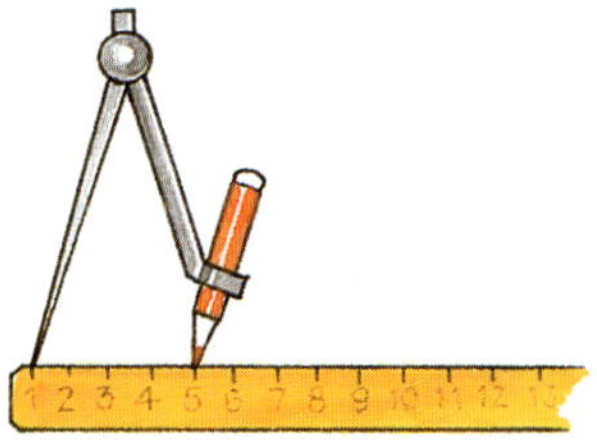

Remember how to draw circles.

Use a ruler to set the compasses to the radius you want.

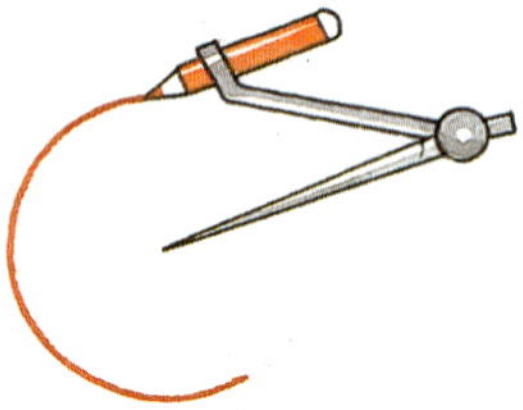

Place the compass point where you want the centre of the circle.

Draw smoothly round it with the pencil.

Measure these circles and draw them.

1.

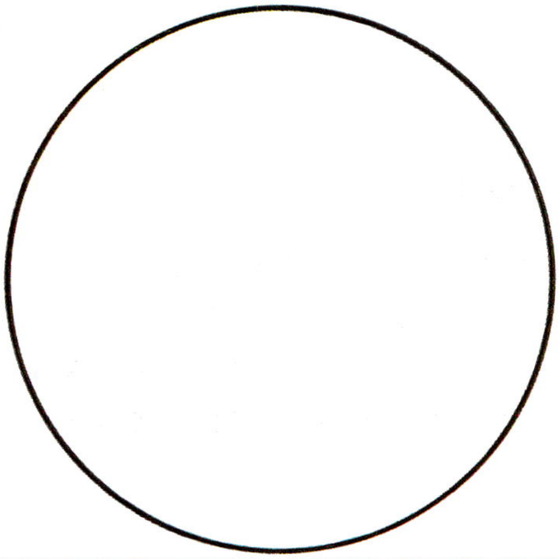

2.

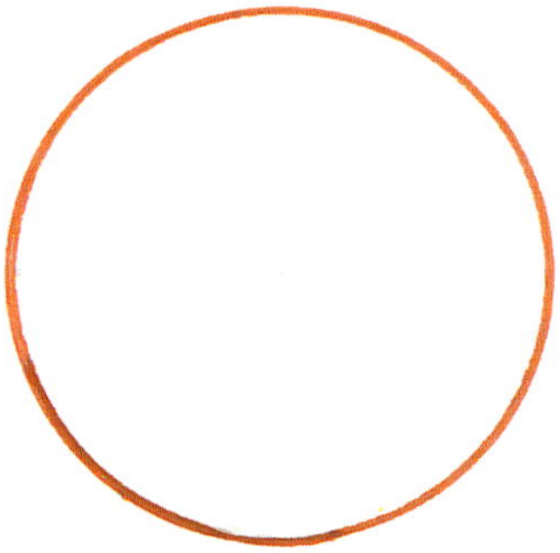

3. Draw a circle with a radius of 5 cm.

4. Draw a circle with a diameter of 7 cm.

---

5. Draw this bear twice as large.

Circles within circles

You will need a pair of compasses, paper and a ruler.

1. Drawing concentric circles.

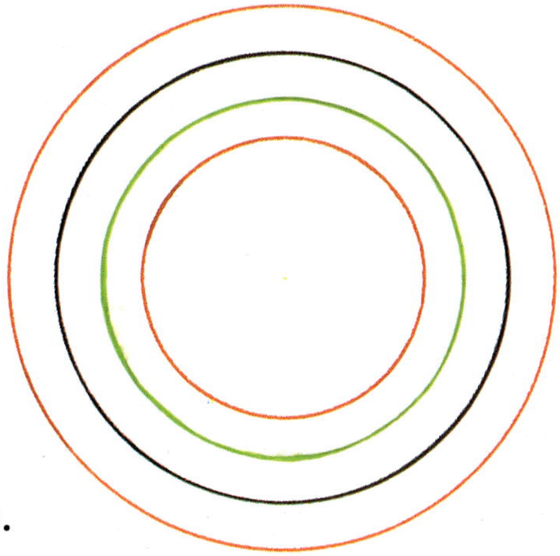

Set your compasses at a radius of 6 cm. Draw a circle. Reduce the radius by 1 cm and draw another circle using the same centre.

Carry on reducing the radius by 1 cm each time and draw more circles inside the first one.

These are called concentric circles.

2. Interference patterns

Try this pattern.

It was made by drawing concentric circles. Then horizontal lines were drawn. The spaces were shaded like a chessboard.

3. Flowers

These flowers were drawn by setting the compasses and drawing a circle. **Without changing the radius setting**, the compasses were 'stepped' around the circumference to make 6 marks. A new circle was drawn at each of the marks, and so on. Try it yourself.

There is more about using compasses on page 55.

Is it a prism?

rectangular prism

triangular prism

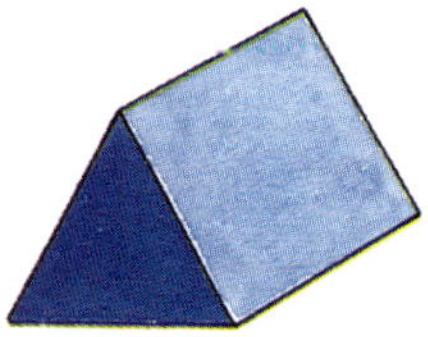

cube

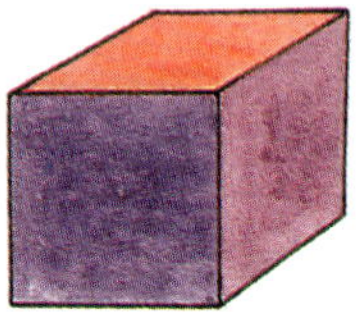

pentagonal prism

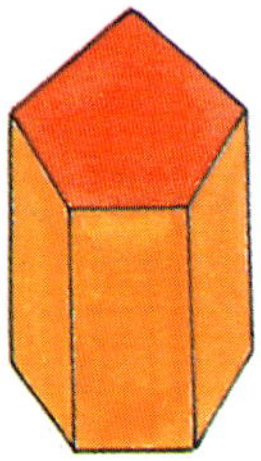

Remember: a prism is a solid shape with identical (congruent) and parallel end faces. If you cut through a prism parallel to the ends, the cross-section is identical (congruent) to the end faces.

Prisms are usually named after the shape of their bases.

The other faces of common prisms are rectangular.

Which of these are prisms?

Look for prisms around the school and at home.
Find as many as you can and make a display.

Making prisms

This is a triangular prism.

The triangular ends measure 4 cm x 4 cm x 4 cm.
The length is 6 cm.

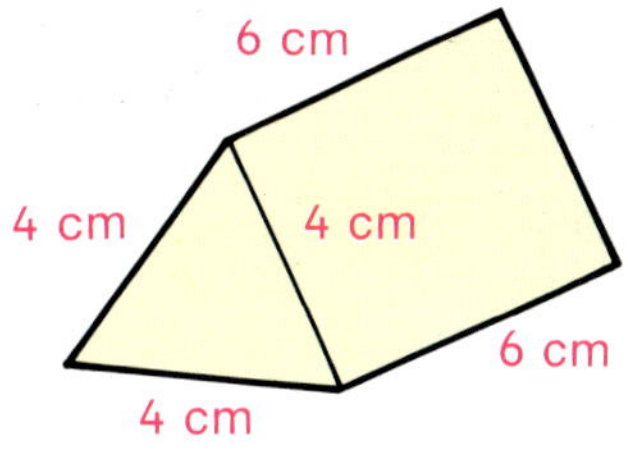

1. Draw the net for this prism and make it.

Make these prisms in the same way.

2. Rectangular prism with end faces 6 cm x 4 cm and 8 cm long.
3. Hexagonal prism with 5 cm edges to the end faces and 10 cm long.

Which of these nets will make a prism?

4. 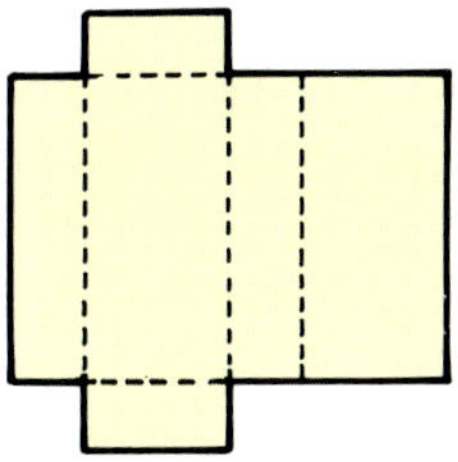

5. 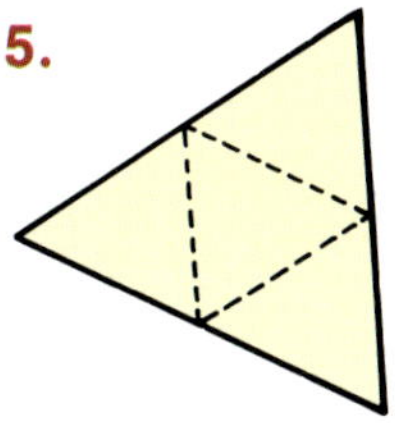

6. 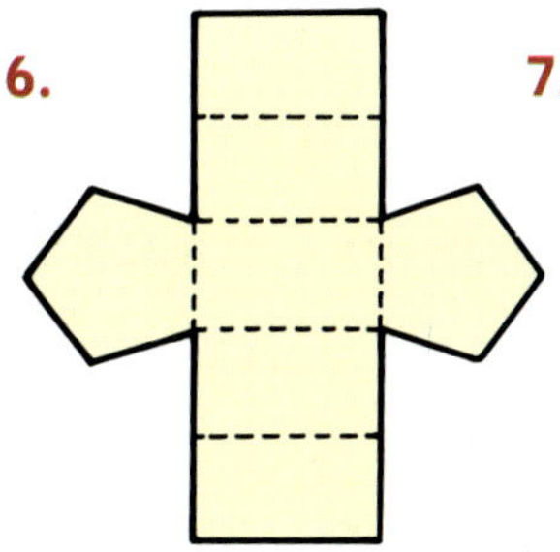

7. 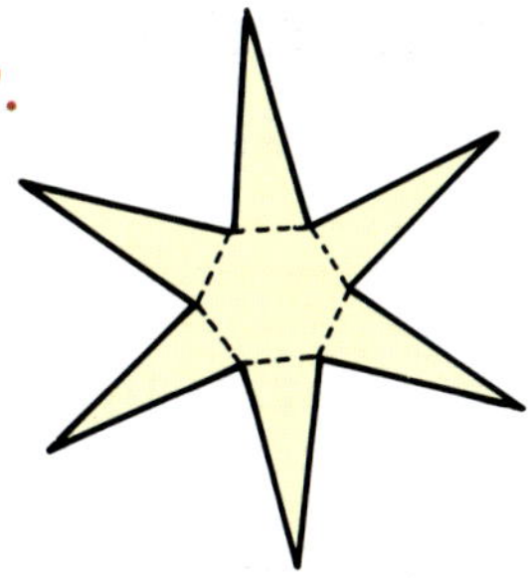

---

8. **Open prisms**

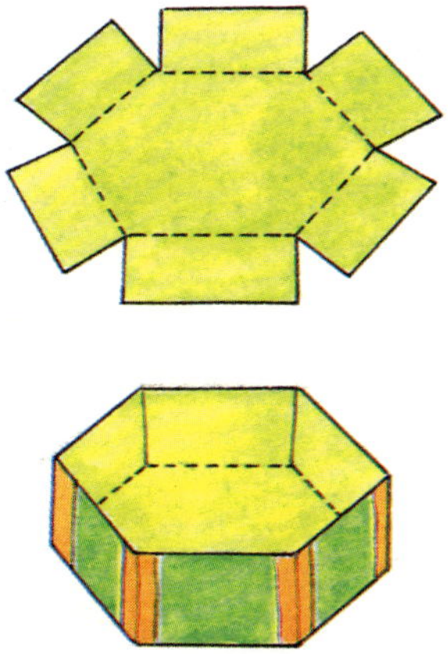

Open prisms can make attractive shallow boxes.
Make this net of a hexagon with 6 shallow tabs.

Fold the tabs up and fix them with sticky tape.
Try other shapes as bases.
Try to make lids for your boxes.

Miles, yards, feet and inches

In Britain, people used to measure all lengths in miles, yards, feet and inches. These are called Imperial measures.

There are:

12 inches in 1 foot

3 feet in 1 yard

and 1760 yards in a mile

Children at school used to have to work these out.

Try them:

How many inches in:

1. 2 feet **2.** 1 yard **3.** 5 yards **4.** 10 feet

5. How many yards in 5 miles?

6. How many feet in a mile?

Comparing Imperial and metric

You will need a ruler marked in inches and a ruler marked in centimetres and millimetres.

Imperial	Metric
1 inch	2 cm 5 mm
2 inches	?
3 inches	?

7. Draw a line 1 inch long.
Measure it in cm and mm.
Make a chart like this. Do the same for lines 2 inches, 3 inches, and so on.

8. Can you find a quick way to change inches to cm and mm?

Measuring in Imperial units

Carpenters would make sketches and charts before making things out of wood. For quickness, they used 'ins' for inches and 'ft' for feet.

Often they needed to use $\frac{1}{2}$ inches.

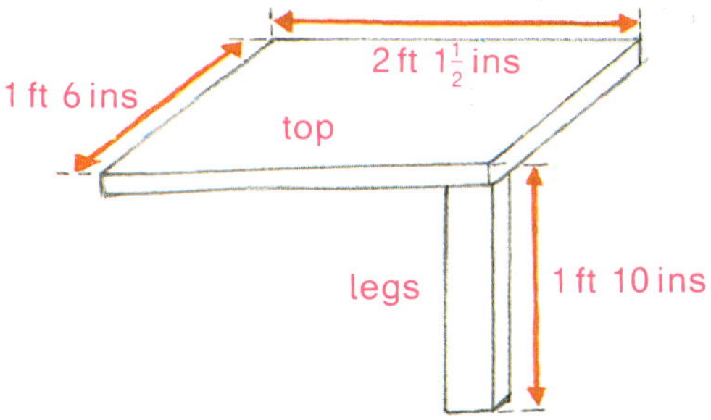

Table

pieces	length	width	thickness
top (1)	2 ft $1\frac{1}{2}$ ins	1 ft 6 ins	$\frac{1}{2}$ ins
legs (4)	1 ft $10\frac{1}{2}$ ins	$1\frac{1}{2}$ ins	$1\frac{1}{2}$ ins

Make your own sketch and chart as if you were going to make these out of wood.

1. your table
2. your chair

---

3. Measure yourself and 5 friends using feet and inches to the nearest inch. Put the measurements in order from tallest to shortest.
4. You will need a metre stick, chalk, a foot ruler.

   With the chalk, draw a line 1 metre long on the playground. Measure it in yards, feet and inches. Make a chart. Do the same for lines 2 metres long, 3 metres long, and so on.
5. Collect examples of Imperial measuring devices like yard sticks and tape measures showing inches, and so on. Make a display.

There is more about Imperial measures on page 60.

Lotions and potions

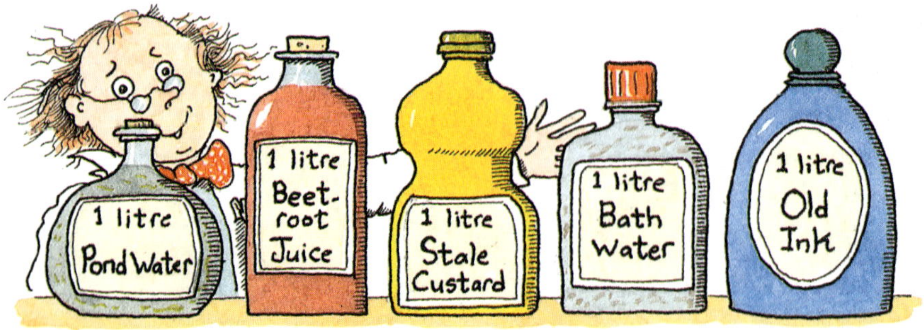

Remember: there are 1000 millilitres in a litre.

The professor makes his own lotions and potions. Here are some of his recipes for lotions.

Write down how much liquid each one makes.

1. Hair Restorer Lotion

   250 ml beetroot juice
   175 ml bath water
   50 ml custard

   Rub on head where hair is required.

2. Wart Reducer Lotion

   350 ml pond water
   50 ml beetroot juice
   150 ml custard
   200 ml ink

   Spread on warts, leave for 7 days.

3. Verruca Killer Lotion

   150 ml beetroot juice
   250 ml custard
   220 ml bath water
   125 ml ink

   Wash feet with lotion twice daily.

4. Nail Strengthening Lotion

   550 ml pond water
   250 ml beetroot juice
   350 ml custard
   425 ml bath water
   375 ml ink

   Dip hands into this for 1 hour.

5. The professor makes each of his recipes. How much of each bottle of ingredients does he have left?

6. Use the rest of the ingredients to invent your own lotion or potion. What is it for? How much liquid do you make?

Do not try this at home.

Using liquids

1. Jennifer has to take 10 ml of her medicine 4 times a day. She has a 250 ml bottle of medicine. How long will it last?

2. A light aircraft burns 75 l of fuel every hour. How many litres of fuel are used on a 3-hour flight?

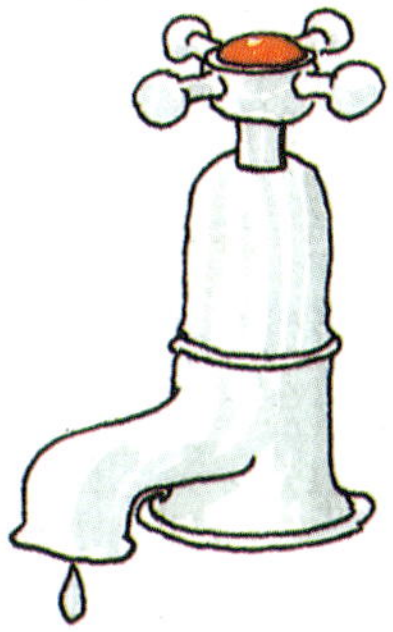

3. A leaky tap drips 1.25 l of water every half-hour. How much is wasted in 5 hours?

4. A Mini Metro uses 1.75 l of petrol every 10 miles. How much does it use to travel 200 miles?

How can you use the buckets to get 4 litres of water?

Length, breadth, height

> Remember: volume is the amount of space a shape occupies.

This cuboid has a length of 4 cm, a breadth of 3 cm and a height of 2 cm.

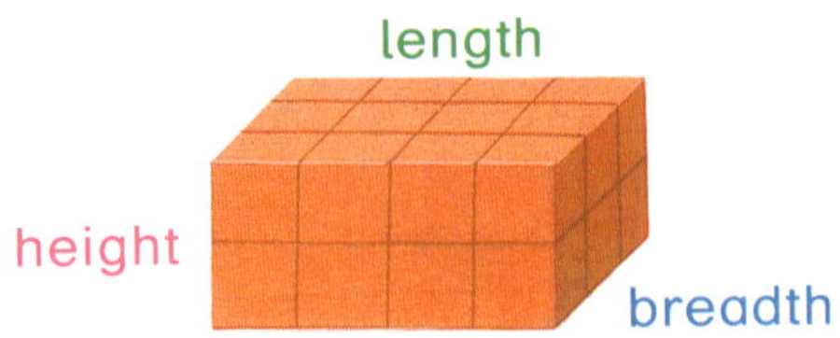

Its volume is 24 cm^3.

4 cm x 3 cm x 2 cm = 24 cm^3.

Length x breadth x height = volume.

Use length x breadth x height to find the volumes of these cuboids.

1.

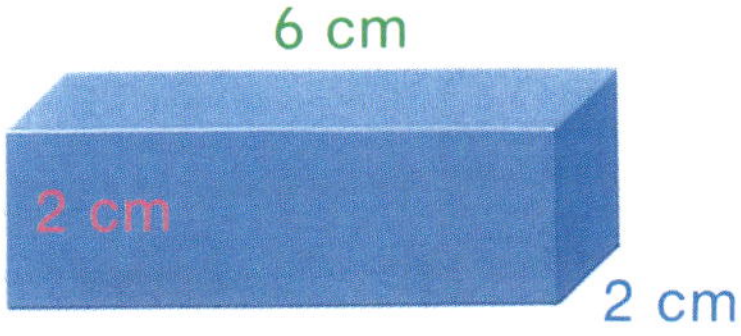

2.

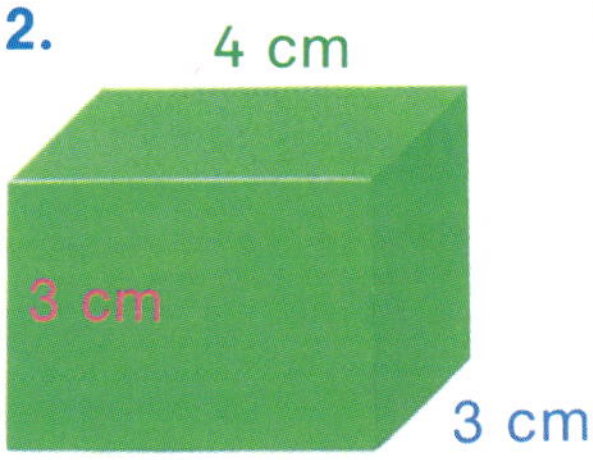

3.

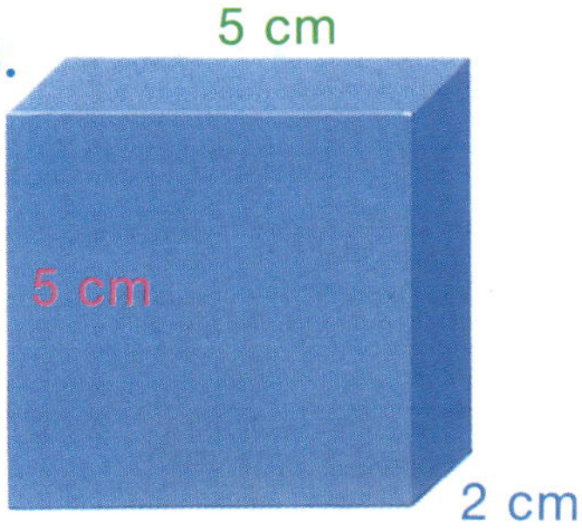

4.

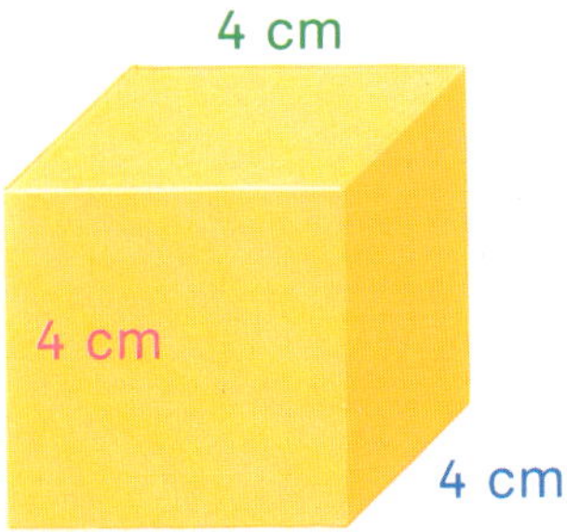

5.

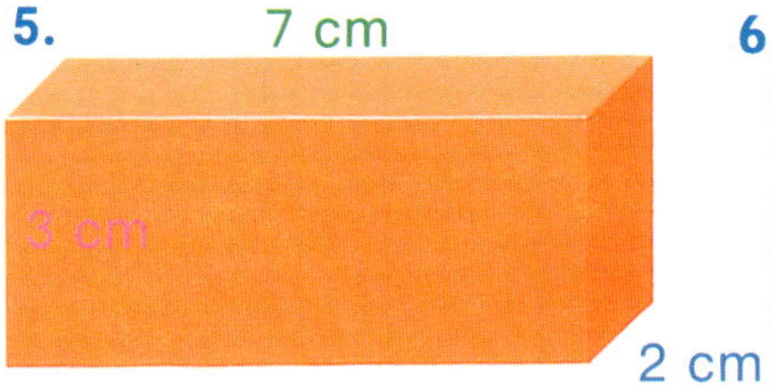

6.

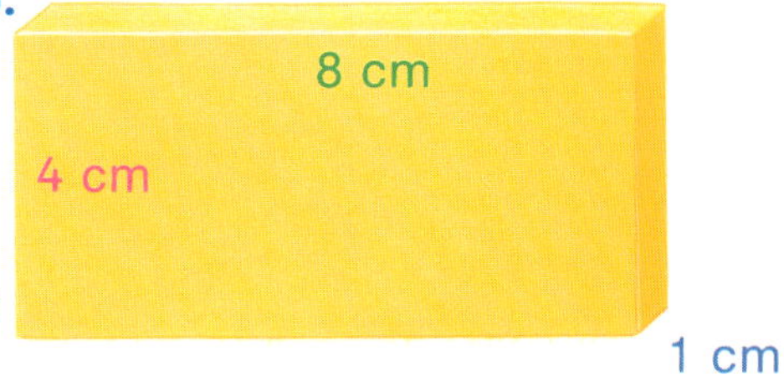

On each of these cuboids, either the length, breadth or height is missing. Write down the missing measurement.

7.

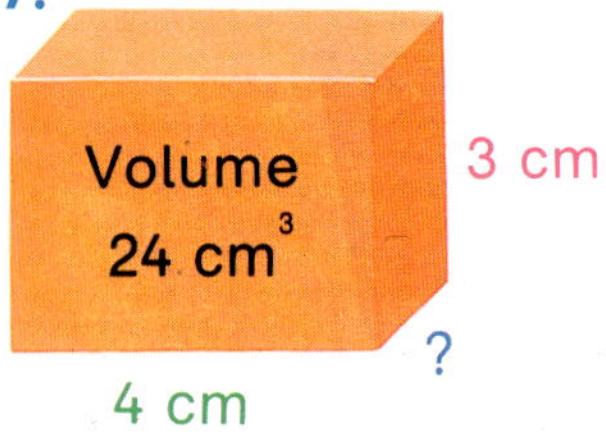

8. length ?
breadth 6 cm
height 2 cm
volume 36 cm^3

9. length 6 cm
breadth 3 cm
height ?
volume 54 cm^3

Finding pairs

These shapes each have a partner with the same volume. Work out the volumes of the shapes. Write down the numbers for each pair.

1.

2.

3.

4.

5.

6.

7.

8.

There is more about volume on page 96.

Nets and boxes

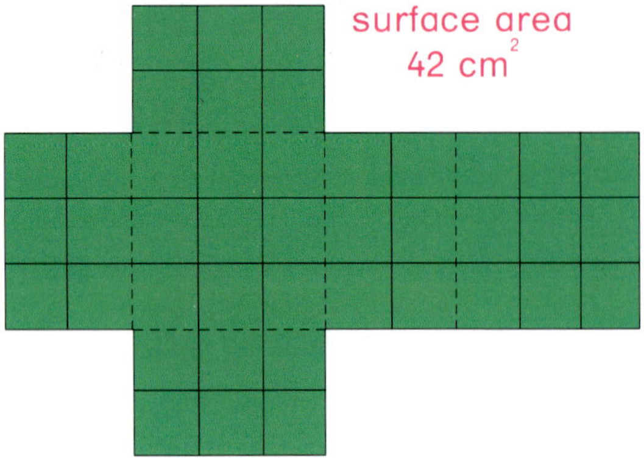

When a box is flattened out to show its net, you can see its whole surface area
Each square on this page represents 1 cm.

Find the surface areas of these nets.

1.

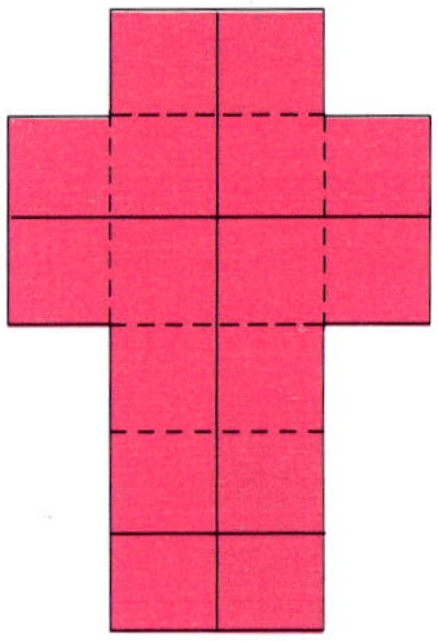

2.

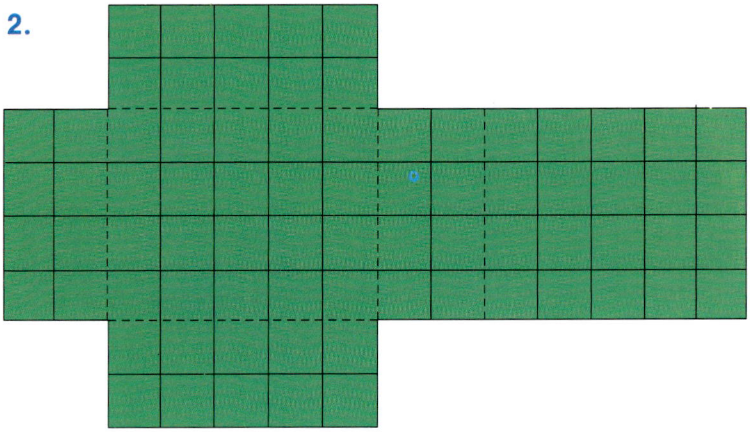

3.

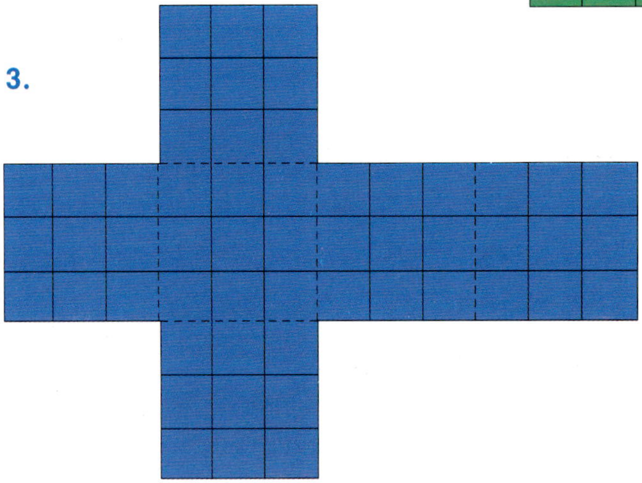

4. Use centimetre squared paper to make a box from net number 3.

How many centimetre cubes can you fit inside it?

Find the surface area

You can work out the surface area of a box by measuring length, breadth and height, and calculating the area of each face.

Remember: a box has 6 faces, so you should have 6 areas to add up to find the total.

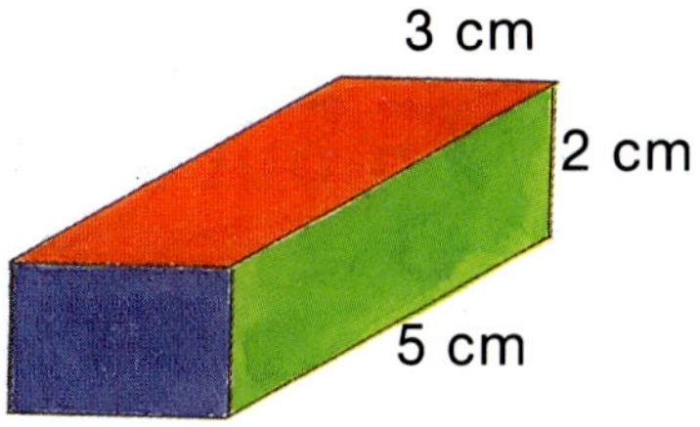

2 red faces
5 cm x 3 cm = 15 cm^2
5 cm x 3 cm = 15 cm^2

2 green faces
5 cm x 2 cm = 10 cm^2
5 cm x 2 cm = 10 cm^2

2 blue faces
3 cm x 2 cm = 6 cm^2
3 cm x 2 cm = 6 cm^2

Total 62 cm^2

Find the surface areas of these boxes.

1.
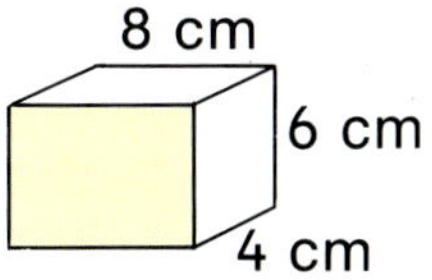

2.
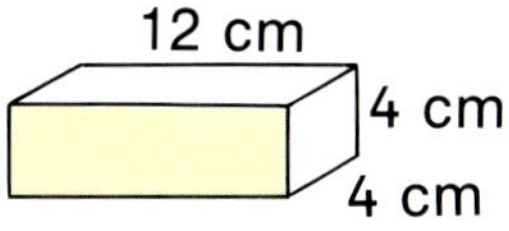

3.
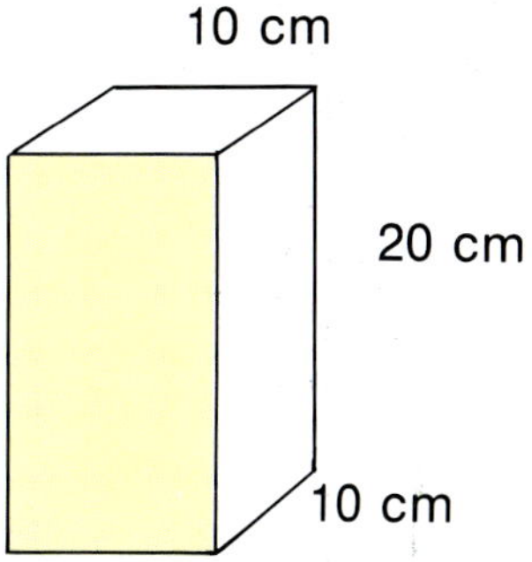

4.
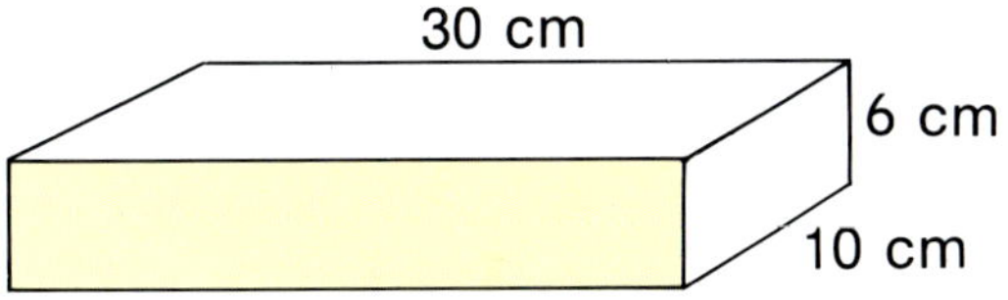

5.
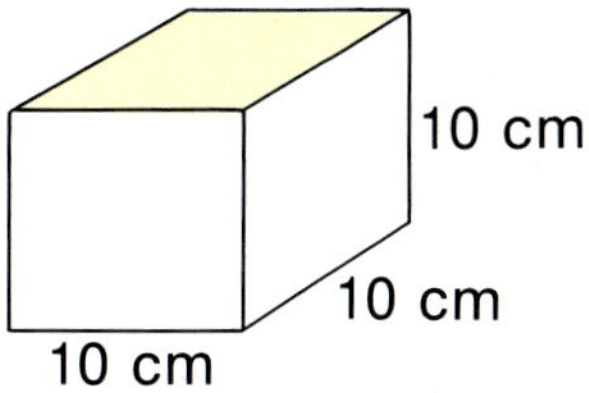

6.
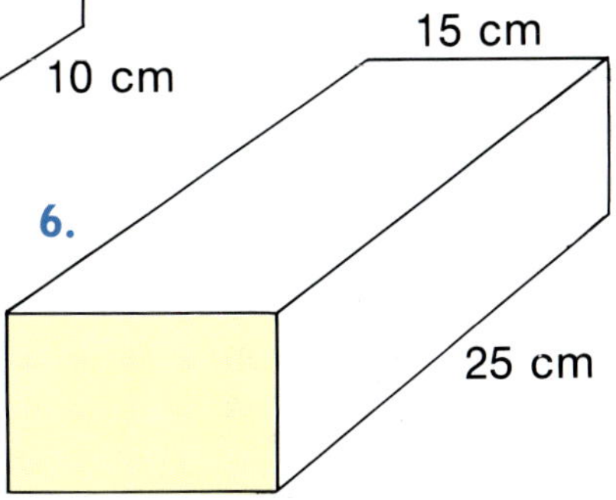

7.
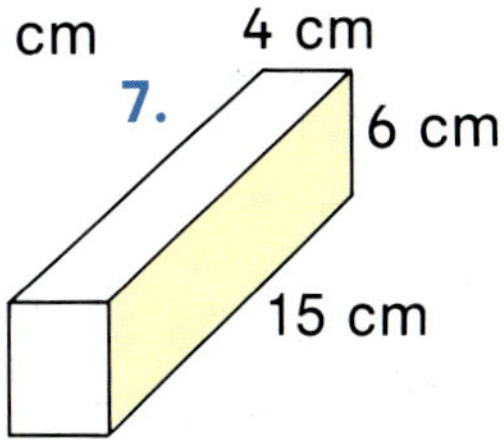

8. If a box has a surface area of 48 cm^2, what **could** its length, breadth and height be?

There is more about area on page 64.

Finding out about capital letters

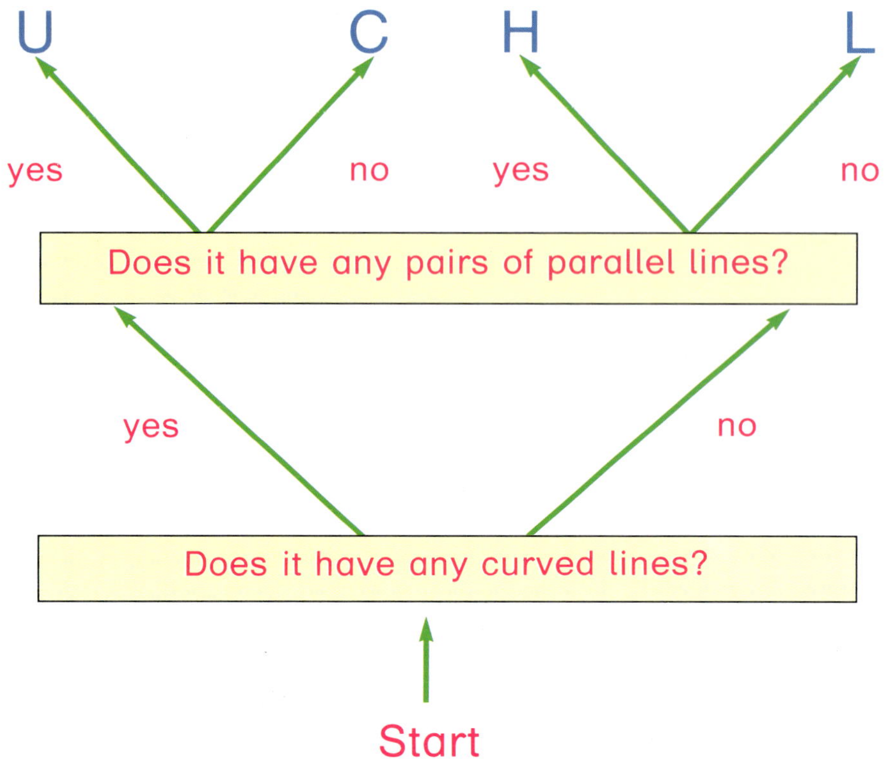

Here is a tree diagram for sorting capital letters.

U, C, H and L have been sorted on to the diagram for you.

1. Draw the diagram and sort the rest of the capital letters on to it.
2. How many letters have curves and parallel lines?
3. How many letters have curves but no parallel lines?
4. Describe the largest group of capital letters.
5. Describe the smallest group of capital letters.

Something has gone wrong!

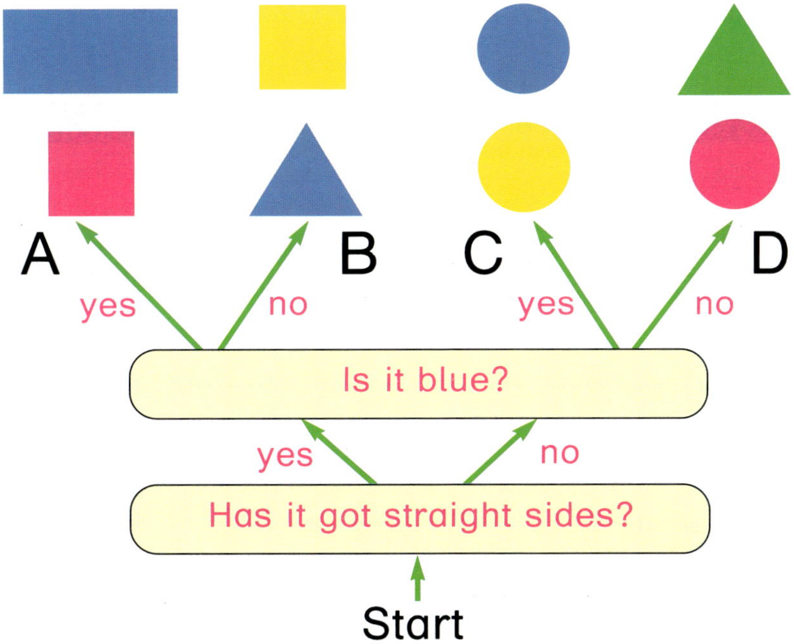

This tree diagram has been used to sort shapes, but some have been sorted wrongly.

1. Which shapes have been wrongly sorted?
2. Sort these shapes. Write where they should be on the diagram. Write A, B, C or D.

Make your own tree diagram

Draw your own tree diagram to sort the children in your class. Use questions like:

Are you a girl? and Are you wearing grey?

There is more about tree diagrams on page 98.

A day on the railway

Here is some information about preserved railways in the West Country.

AVON

Avon Valley Railway, Bitton Railway Station, Willsbridge, Bristol. BS15 6ED. Tel. Timetable Enquiries (0272) 327296 Other Enquiries (0272) 40990. On A431 Midway between Bristol & Bath. Opening Times 11.00 am to 5.00 pm. Open Site open weekends throughout year. Steaming: 1st Sun each Month & Bank Holidays March to Nov. Special Events 26 to 30 June, Schools Week. 25, 26 Nov, 2,3,9,10,16,17,23,26,30,31 Dec. 1 Jan 1990. Santa Specials. (1) (SG) ☕ ♿ (P) ≠ BRISTOL TEMPLE MEADS (5)

Bristol Harbour Railway, Bristol Industrial Museum, Princes Wharf, Bristol. BS1 4RN. Tel. (0272) 299771 ext. 290. Bristol City Docks. Opening Times 12.00 noon to 6.00 pm. Open As advertised locally. All Bank Holiday weekends except Good Friday, Christmas & New Year. (½) (SG) (P) ≠ BRISTOL TEMPLE MEADS (1)

CORNWALL

Bodmin & Wenford Railway, Bodmin General Station, Lostwitheal Road, Bodmin, Cornwall. PL31 1AQ. Tel. Timetable Enquiries (0208) 77963 Other Enquiries (0208) 74878/75611. On B3269, Lostwithiel Road. ¼ mile South of Bodmin Centre. Opening Times 10.30 am to 5.00 pm. Open Museum open daily 1 May to 1 Oct. Operating 26,27 Mar, 30 Apr, 1,28,29 May. Sun, Wed, Thur, 11 June to 8 July. Sun to Thurs, 9 July to 17 Sept. (3) (SG) ☕ ♿ (P) ≠ BODMIN PARKWAY (3)

Launceston Steam Railway, St. Thomas Road, Launceston, Cornwall. PL15 8DA. Tel. (0566) 5665. Just down the hill from Launceston Castle. Opening Times 11.00 am to 5.00 pm. Open 24 to 27 Mar, Daily 29 May to 1 Oct. Special Events 2,3,9,10,16,17,23,24 Dec. Santa Specials. (2) (NG) ☕ (P) ≠ PLYMOUTH (25)

DEVON

Buckfastleigh & Totnes Steam Railway, The Station, Buckfastleigh, Devon. TQ11 0DZ. Tel. Timetable Enquiries (0364) 42338 Other Enquiries (0364) 43536. Off A38. Buckfastleigh turn. Opening Times 10.00 am to 5.30 pm. Open see timetable. (7) (SG) ☕ ♿ (P) ≠ TOTNES (6)

Paignton & Dartmouth Steam Railway, Queens Park Station, Paignton, Devon. Tel. Timetable Enquiries (0803) 555872 Other Enquiries (0803) 553760. Adjacent to Paignton BR Station. Opening Times 9.00 am to 5.30 pm. Open see timetable. Special Events Dec. Santa Specials, please enquire for details. (7) (SG) ☕ ♿ (P) ≠ PAIGNTON

Plym Valley Railway, Marsh Mills Station, Coypool Road, Marsh Mills, Plymouth, Devon. PL7 4NL. Tel. (0752) 330478. On B3416 ¼ mile from A38 Marsh Mills roundabout. Opening Times 10.00 am to dusk. Open Railway under construction. Steam and diesel operation on selected weekends. Enquire for details. Special Events Easter & Sept. Open Days, enquire for details. (¼) (SG) ☕ (P) ≠ PLYMOUTH (3)

Tiverton Museum, St. Andrew Street, Tiverton, Devon. EX16 6PH. Tel. (0884) 256295. In centre of Tiverton. Opening Times 10.30 am to 4.30 pm. Open Mons to Sats (Inc. Bank Holidays) 30 Jan. to 22 Dec. (SG) (BG) | ♿ (P) ≠ TIVERTON PARKWAY (5)

KEY TO SYMBOLS

- ♿ – facilities for the Disabled (Prior phone call advised).
- ≠ – Nearest Station - BR unless otherwise indicated (approximate mileage distance where appropriate between Stations and Steam Centre given in brackets)
- (P) – Car Parking
- (1) – Length of Operating Line (miles)
- ☕ – Light Refreshments
- 🍷 – Licenced Bar
- 🍴 – Special Dining Car Train (advanced booking essential)
- (NG) – Narrow Gauge
- (SG) – Standard Gauge (4' 8½")
- (BG) – Broad Gauge

Plan your day out

Use the information on page 36 to answer these questions.

1. What time does the Launceston Steam Railway open?
2. Can you visit the Tiverton Museum on a Sunday?
3. List all the railways which have facilities for the disabled.
4. It takes you $1\frac{1}{2}$ hours to reach the Paignton and Dartmouth Steam Railway. What time would you have to leave home to arrive for opening time? If you stay until closing time, what time will you get home?
5. How far is Bodmin Parkway Station from the Bodmin and Wenford Railway?
6. How long is the railway line on the Buckfastleigh and Totnes Steam Railway?
7. In which season of the year is the Schools Week on the Avon Valley Railway?
8. How far is the Plym Valley Railway from the Marsh Mills Roundabout?

Subtraction on a number line

Sometimes drawing a number line can help to find the difference between two numbers.

For example, Sarah drew this for 423 – 378

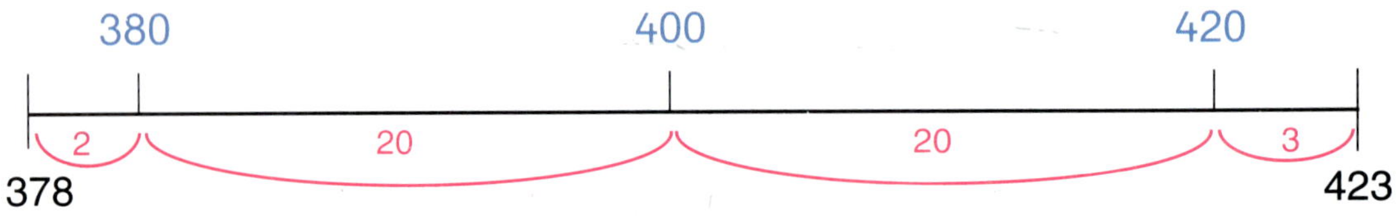

She added on from 378, 2 + 20 + 20 + 3, to get the answer 45.

Try drawing number lines to find these differences.

1. 692 – 545 **2.** 321 – 267 **3.** 816 – 797 **4.** 433 – 312

5. 924 – 799 **6.** 211 – 158 **7.** 572 – 451 **8.** 734 – 686

---

9. Jane spilled coffee on this list of price changes. Write out a new list for her.

Item	old price	new price	price rise
Fridge	£325	£359	
Washer/Drier	£437		£125
Cooker	£645		£254
Microwave	£197	£215	
Dishwasher		£385	£98

Coded subtractions

Each letter of the alphabet can stand for a digit from 0 to 9.

a	b	c	d	e	f	g	h	i	j	k	l	m	n	o	p	q	r	s	t	u	v	w	x	y	z
0	1	2	3	4	5	6	7	8	9	0	1	2	3	4	5	6	7	8	9	0	1	2	3	4	5

1. Subtract abc from def. Write the number.
2. What number is the difference between pod and pea?
3. Write a code for the answer to 471 – 289.
4. What number is the difference between him and her?
5. Subtract lmn from hij. Write the number.
6. Write a code for the answer to 689 – 302.
7. What number is the difference between dog and cat?
8. Subtract wxy from stu. Write the number.
9. Write a code for the answer to 842 – 377.
10. What number is the difference between car and bus?

Make up your own coded subtractions.

Missing digit subtractions

In these subtractions some of the digits are missing.
Write them out with all the digits.

11. 439 – 1□6 = 31□
12. 5□7 – 263 = □74
13. □25 – 532 = 1□3
14. 86□ – □45 = 623

There is more about subtraction on page 72.

Dividing everyday numbers

1. How many children in this class?
2. Can they be split into groups of 6, without leaving anyone out?
3. Try to split them into groups of 2, 3, 4, 5, 7, 8, 9 and 10. Which numbers leave some children out?
4. Try this with the number of children in your class.

All about 100

5. What is one half of 100?
6. What is a quarter of 100?
7. Can you divide 100 exactly into eighths?
8. Find all the numbers which divide 100 exactly.
9. Try to find all the numbers which divide 50, 75 and 25 or any other 2-digit numbers exactly.

Zig-zag number track

0 1 2 3 4 5 6 7 8 9 10 11 12 13 14 15 16 17 18 19 20 21 22 23 24 25
26 27 28 29 30 31 32

1. Start at zero. How many jumps of 5 to reach 65?

2. Start at zero. Jump in sevens to 84. Write each number you jump on to.

58 57 56 55 54 53 52 51 50 49 48 47 46 45 44 43 42 41 40 39 38 37 36 35 34 33
59 60 61 62 63 64

3. Start at 90. Jump back in sixes. How many jumps to reach zero?

4. Start at 96. Jump back in eights. How many jumps to reach zero?

65 66 67 68 69 70 71 72 73 74 75 76 77 78 79 80 81 82 83 84 85 86 87 88 89 90
91 92 93 94 95 96 97 98 99 100

5. Start at 97. Jump back in nines.
How many whole jumps to reach zero?
How many between the last jump and zero?

6. Start at 80. Jump back in fives.
How many jumps to zero?

7. Design your own number track to 100. Use different colours to show jumps of 5, jumps of 6, and so on.

8. **Strawberry picking**

Teams of children picked strawberries. After 5 minutes, each team stopped and shared the strawberries out. Which team got the best share for each person?

In Team A, 5 children picked 66 strawberries.
In Team B, 6 children picked 72 strawberries.
In Team C, 4 children picked 50 strawberries.
In Team D, 7 children picked 87 strawberries.

Beyond 9999

Start at 9999. Add, or count on, these numbers.
Write the answers.

1. 2 **2.** 10 **3.** 125 **4.** 491

5. 1320 **6.** 2357 **7.** 5215 **8.** 8339

Write these numbers using numerals.

9. Twelve thousand three hundred and eighty-six.

10. Thirty-five thousand eight hundred and fifty.

11. Seventy thousand five hundred and ninety-nine.

12. One hundred and ten thousand six hundred and forty-five.

13. Two hundred and fifty-seven thousand three hundred and thirty-eight.

14. Eight hundred and fifty-two thousand one hundred and sixty-four.

Write these numbers as words.

15. 59 802 **16.** 45 195

17. 120 650 **18.** 999 999

What is it worth?

125 609

The numeral **5** in this number is worth 5000, because of its place in the thousands column.

Write what the red numerals are worth in these numbers.

1. 125 609	**2.** 125 609	**3.** 125 609	**4.** 125 609
5. 58 463	**6.** 58 463	**7.** 58 463	**8.** 58 463
9. 752 186	**10.** 752 186	**11.** 752 186	**12.** 752 186

13.

A bookworm tunnelled its way through the entire 15 volumes of a set of encyclopaedias. Each volume had 1856 pages. How many pages did the bookworm tunnel through?

There is more about big numbers on page 76.

Hundredths

These pictures show tenths and hundredths and how to write them as decimals.

three tenths

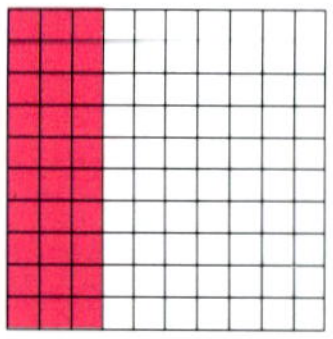

ones	tenths
0 •	3

0.3

five hundredths

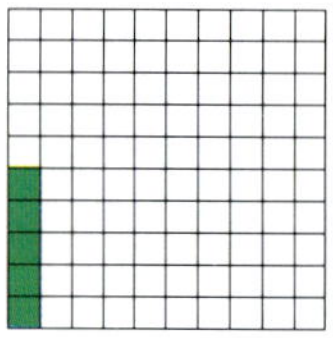

ones	tenths	hundredths
0 •	0	5

0.05

thirty-five hundredths

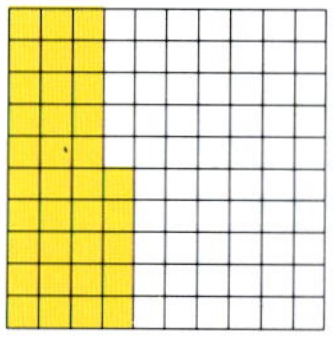

ones	tenths	hundredths
0 •	3	5

0.35

Write the decimals shown by these pictures.
Draw a chart if it helps.

1. 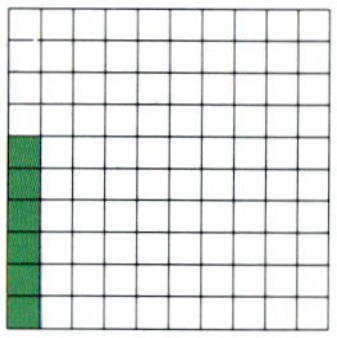

2. 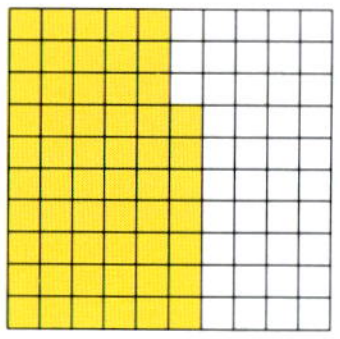

3. 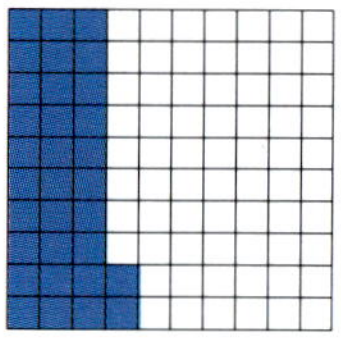

4. 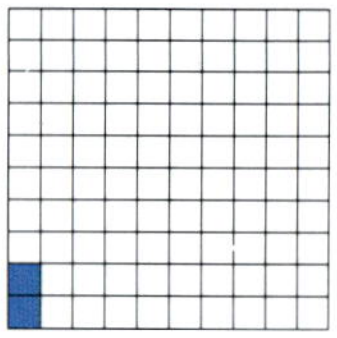

5. 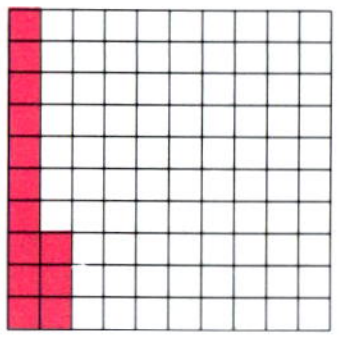

6. 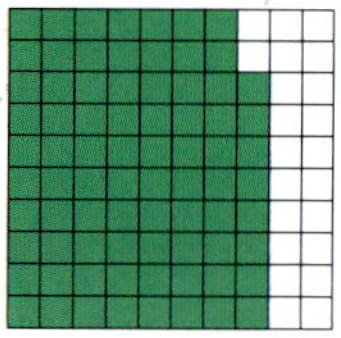

Use squares marked in hundreds. Colour these amounts.

7.

ones	tenths	hundredths
0 •	0	7

8.

ones	tenths	hundredths
0 •	4	5

9.

ones	tenths	hundredths
0 •	1	8

10. 0.09 **11.** 0.14 **12.** 0.72

Decimal money

> Remember: 100p = £1.00
> 150p = £1.50
> 105p = £1.05

Write these amounts of pennies as pounds (£).

1. 175p **2.** 225p **3.** 309p **4.** 580p

5. 1260p **6.** 2505p **7.** 1995p **8.** 4999p

Write these amounts of money as pennies.

9. £4.50 **10.** £15.25 **11.** £12.05 **12.** £29.99

---

13. Alison measured her height.

It was 136 cm. She wrote it in two ways:

name	cm	m
Alison	136 cm	1.36 m

Measure your height and four of your friends. Make a chart. Write the heights in two ways.

14. Use a square marked in hundredths.

Create a design by colouring 0.24 in one colour and 0.76 in another.

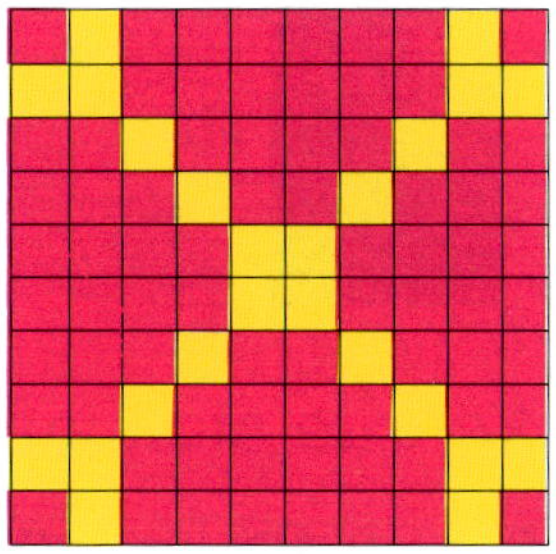

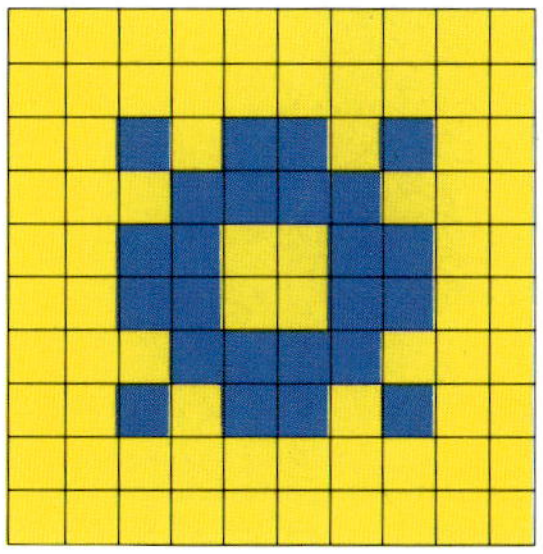

Comparing decimals

0.12 > 0.09

0.12 is greater than 0.09

> means 'is greater than'.

If the tenths are the same, look at the hundredths.

0.22 is less than 0.28

< means 'is less than'.

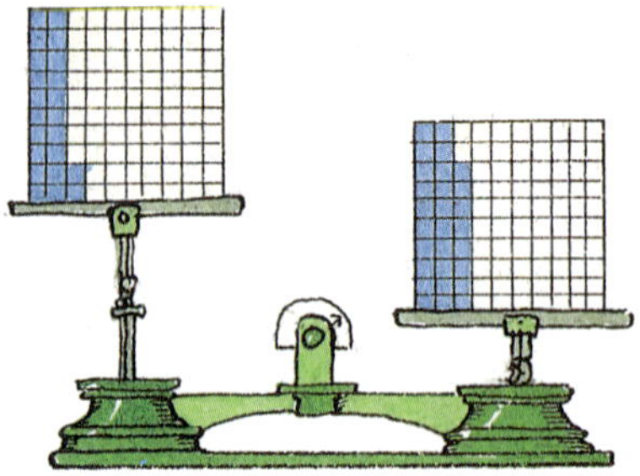

0.22 < 0.28

Sometimes numbers are equal.

0.3 equals 0.30

= means 'equals'.

0.3 = 0.30

How much is coloured? Use >, <, or = to make true statements.

1. 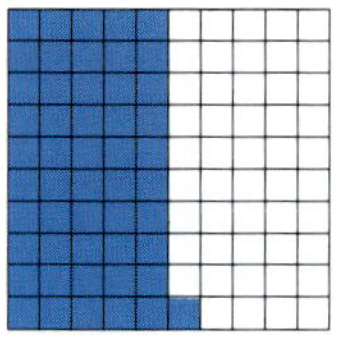 0.51 0.15 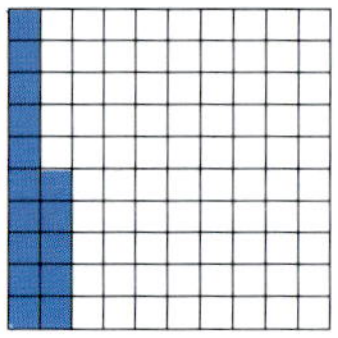

2. 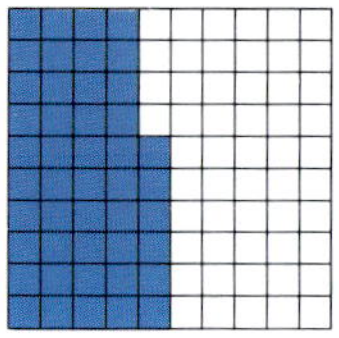 0.46 0.7 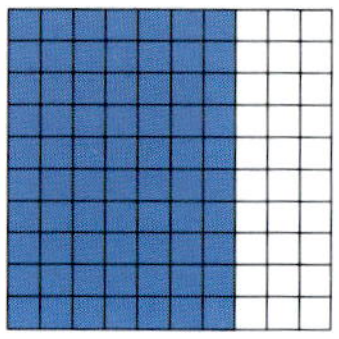

3. 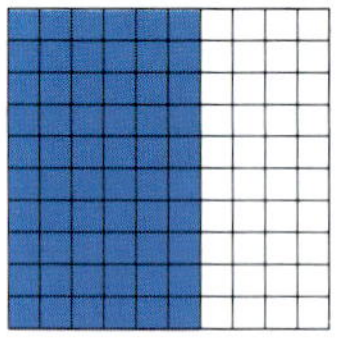 0.60 0.06 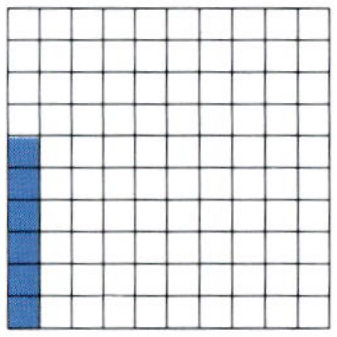

4. 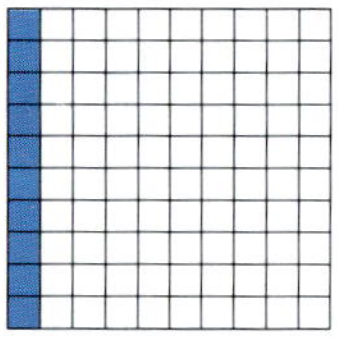 0.1 0.8 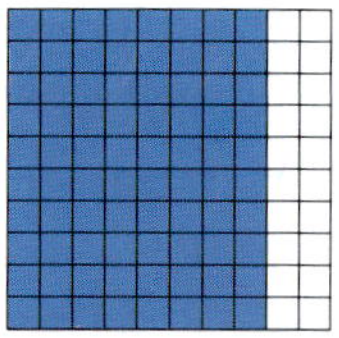

5. 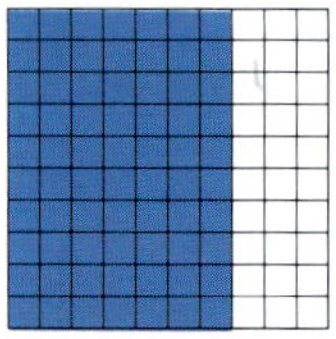 0.7 0.70 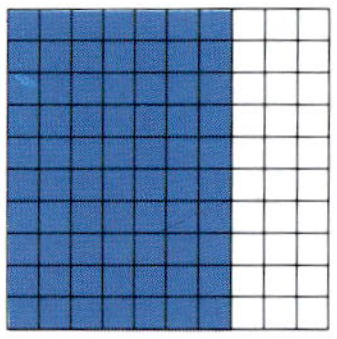

6. 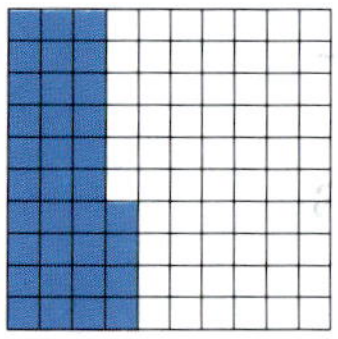 0.34 0.3 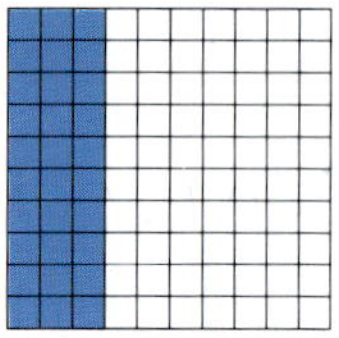

Write >, < or = to make true statements.

7. 0.26 0.52 **8.** 0.13 0.13 **9.** 0.64 0.46 **10.** 0.07 0.7

Putting decimals in order

Write the next three numbers in these series.

1. 0.26, 0.27, 0.28, _____ , _____ , _____
2. 1.96, 1.97, 1.98, _____ , _____ , _____
3. 6.25, 6.24, 6.23, _____ , _____ , _____
4. 8.04, 8.03, 8.02, _____ , _____ , _____

Put these numbers in order from least to greatest.

5. 2.26, 1.85, 2.9, 1.35
6. 1.04, 0.40, 1.01, 1.4
7. 2.79, 5.12, 2.17, 1.38
8. 1.25, 3.03, 2.71, 1.48

Put these lists in order from greatest to least.

9.

APPLETISE 1 LTR	1.39
APPLETISE 1 LTR	1.39
MINERAL WATER	0.69
MINERAL WATER	0.69
L/CAL MAYONNAISE	1.09
JS FROMAGE FRAIS	0.45
JS FRUIT DUET	0.32
JS SATSUMA/JUICE	0.38
JS APRICOT HALV	0.52
JS BLACKBERRIES	0.50
JS HALF FAT MILK	0.30
JS GRANARY LOAF	0.65

10.

BATHROOM ACCESSORIES	
Gold-plated mirror – diam. 18 ins.	
Order 365-759	*£22.99*
Tumbler and holder	
Order 365-757	*£ 9.50*
Soap dish	
Order 365-756	*£10.99*
Shelf – 20 ins	
Order 365-755	*£14.99*
Towel rail – 24 ins	
Order 365-753	*£14.95*
Towel ring	
Order 365-754	*£ 9.95*
Toilet roll holder	
Order 365-752	*£ 9.99*
Toilet brush/holder	
Order 365-758	*£24.99*

Rounding money

It helps to work out a bill quickly if you 'round' the amounts. If the amounts on the bill were £1.99 and £1.45,

£1.99 rounds up to £2.00 £1.45 rounds down to £1.00

The approximate cost is £3.00. (It is really £3.44.)

11. Use the food bill in Question 9 above. Round all the prices up or down. What is the approximate total cost?

    Now use a calculator to add up the real bill. How close are the two answers?

Mixed numbers and fractions

How many burgers are there?

$$1 + 1 + \frac{1}{2} = 2\frac{1}{2}$$

$$\frac{2}{2} + \frac{2}{2} + \frac{1}{2} = \frac{5}{2}$$

$2\frac{1}{2}$ is a mixed number.

$\frac{5}{2}$ is a fraction greater than 1.

How much is coloured? Write the answer in two ways.

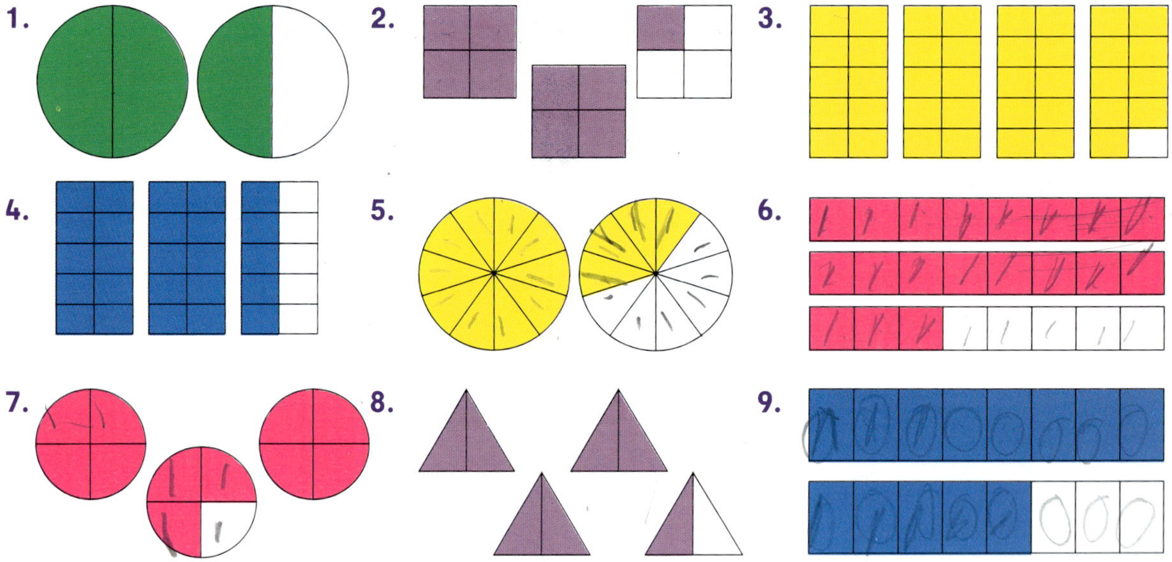

Draw your own pictures to show these mixed numbers and fractions.

10. $2\frac{1}{2}$

11. $\frac{5}{4}$

12. $1\frac{2}{3}$

13. $3\frac{1}{8}$

14. $\frac{11}{10}$

15. $\frac{12}{5}$

Real life problems

Solve these problems. Draw pictures to help you.

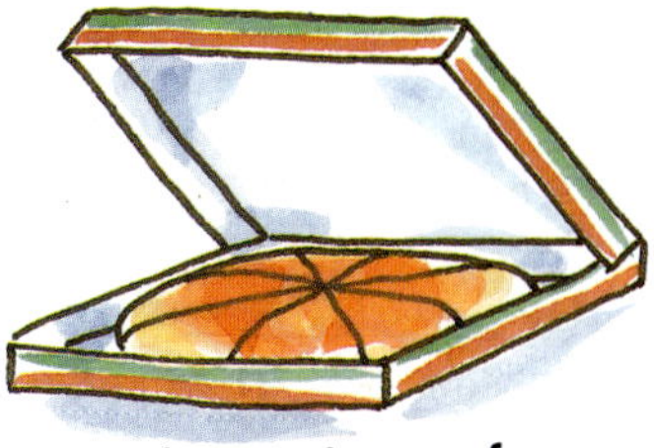

1. The Stone family ordered 2 pizzas. Each pizza was cut into eighths. The family ate 15 pieces. What fraction of the pizzas did they eat?

2. Steve picked some tomatoes from his garden. When he cut them into quarters he had 12 pieces. How many tomatoes did he pick?

3. Four people ordered 5 chapatis with their curry. How much did each person get if they were shared exactly?

4. Four oranges were cut into quarters for the eleven members of the football team. At half time, each player had one piece. How much was left?

5. Three cakes were cut up for the party. There were fifteen guests and each had a fair share. What fraction was each cake cut into?

Write the mixed number.

6. If  is 1, then  is?

7. If  is 1, then 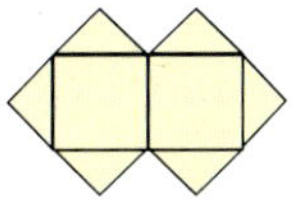 is?

8. If  is 1, then 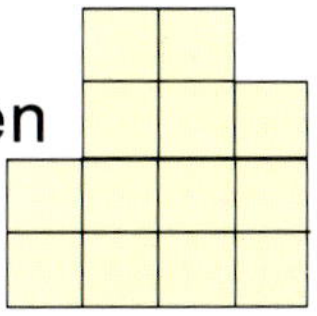 is?

9. If 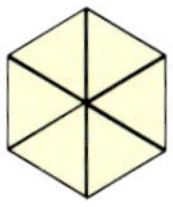 is 1, then 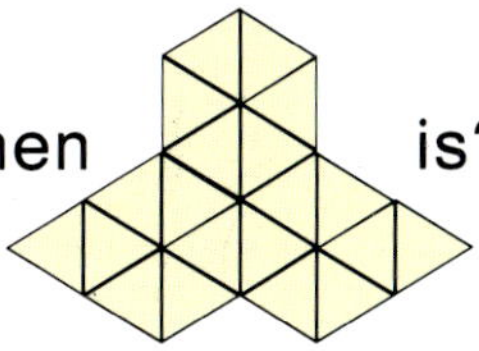 is?

10. Make up some similar puzzles for a friend to try.

Calculator check

Remember: You can check the answer to a multiplication by using its inverse operation.

The inverse operation for multiplication is division.

Is this correct? 63 x 24 = 1512

Check by dividing: 1512 ÷ 24 = 63

Check these multiplications by dividing. Use your calculator. Write **correct** or **incorrect**.

1. 52 x 35 = 1820
2. 67 x 18 = 1256
3. 27 x 49 = 1423
4. 42 x 28 = 1176
5. 48 x 37 = 1776
6. 39 x 56 = 2254

Make some multiplications for a friend to check. Put in some with deliberately wrong answers.

7. **Four fours are ...**

Make all the numbers from 1 to 10 but only use fours. You can use +, –, x, ÷ , = and brackets.

Here are two ideas for making 1 and 2.

4 ÷ 4 = 1

(4 + 4) ÷ 4 = 2

If you want to make it harder, try using exactly four fours each time. For example, (4 + 4 – 4) ÷ 4 = 1

Calculator chains

Remember: negative numbers are numbers below zero. We write them to the left of zero on the number line.

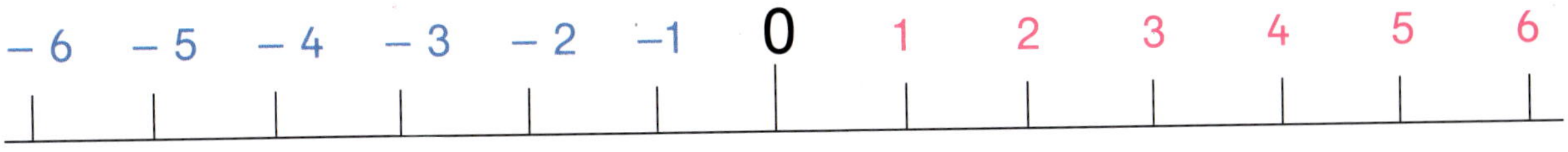

You may wish to use a calculator to help with this number chain.

	key presses	display
Put a negative number into the calculator display.	− 7 =	7.-
If it is odd, subtract 3.	− 3 =	10.-
If it is even, halve it.	÷ 2 =	5.-
If it is odd, subtract 3.	− 3 =	8.-
If it is even, halve it.	÷ 2 =	4.-

1. Continue with this chain. What happens?

2. Try other negative numbers with this chain. What happens?

---

3. Decimals and square roots

Remember: the square root key on your calculator looks like this √

Put any number into your calculator.
Press the √ (square root key) once.
Write down the number in the display.
It might be a decimal number.
Keep pressing the square root key.
Where does the chain appear to be leading?

key	display
20	20
√	4.4721359
√	2.1147425
√	1.4542154
√	1.2059085
√	1.0981386
√	1.047021
	↓

Chains of numbers

Remember: you can set up a constant function on your calculator.

Numbers can grow by repeating the same number operation many times.

1 (+2) 3 (+2) 5 (+2) 7 (+2) 9 (+2) 11

Or they can get smaller. Notice there are two operations here.

15 (−1) 14 (−2) 12 (−1) 11 (−2) 9 (−1) 8 (−2)

Discover the hidden operations in these chains and continue them to their 10th number.

1. 4, 7, 10, 13, 16, ...

2. 42, 38, 34, 30, 26 ...

3. 3, 4, 8, 9, 18, 19 ...

4. 2, 4, 8, 16, 32 ...

Find the longest chain

Start with a 2-digit number. 84

Multiply the two digits. 8 x 4 = 32

Multiply the two digits of the result. 3 x 2 = 6

This chain has three steps, 84 → 32 → 6

Try this with lots of 2-digit numbers.

5. What is the longest chain you can find?

6. What is the shortest chain you can find?

7. What end numbers can be made?

8. What end numbers cannot be made?

Some more number chains to investigate

Where does the chain end?

Start with any number. 17

If it is odd ... add 1. 17 + 1 = 18

If it is even ... halve it. 18 ÷ 2 = 9

Carry on:

9 + 1, 10 ÷ 2, 5 + 1, 6 ÷ 2, 3 → ?

1. Where does this chain end?
2. Try lots of other starting numbers. Where do their chains end?

---

7 times table digits

Start with a 2-digit multiple of 7 →	28
Multiply the ones digit by 5 →	8 x 5 = 40
Add the tens digit to the result →	40 + 2 = 42
Multiply the ones digit by 5 again →	2 x 5 = 10
Add the tens digit to the result →	10 + 4 = 14
	↓
	?

3. Continue this chain. Where does it end?
4. Try other multiples of 7. What do you notice?

Adding and squaring

Start with any 2-digit number.	25
Add the digits.	2 + 5 = 7
Square the result.	7 x 7 = 49
	↓
	?

5. Carry on with this chain. What happens?
6. Try this with lots of different 2-digit starting numbers. What happens in each sequence?

Drawing right-angled triangles

You will need a ruler, a pencil and a set square.

The base is 12 cm and the perpendicular is 24 cm.

If you know the length of the base and perpendicular of a right-angled triangle, you can draw it with a set square.

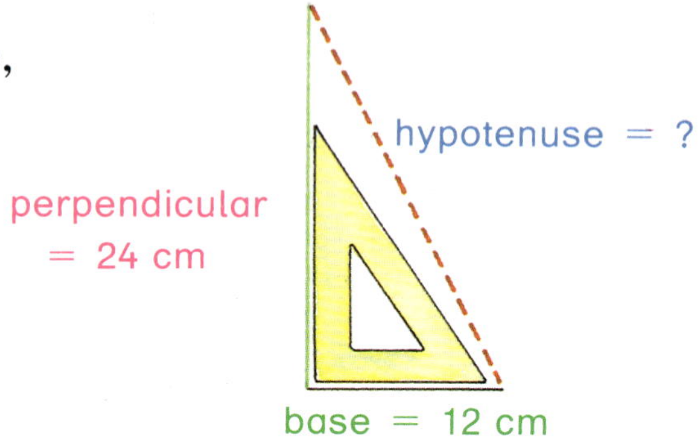

First draw the **base** (12 cm) and use the set square for the right-angled corner.

Then draw the **perpendicular** (24 cm).

Finally draw the hypotenuse.

Draw right-angled triangles using these pairs of measurements. Write the length of the hypotenuse.

1. base 3 cm
   perpendicular 4 cm
2. base 5 cm
   perpendicular 12 cm
3. base 2.5 cm
   perpendicular 6 cm
4. base 6 cm
   perpendicular 8 cm

Mirror images

Draw the mirror images of these triangles

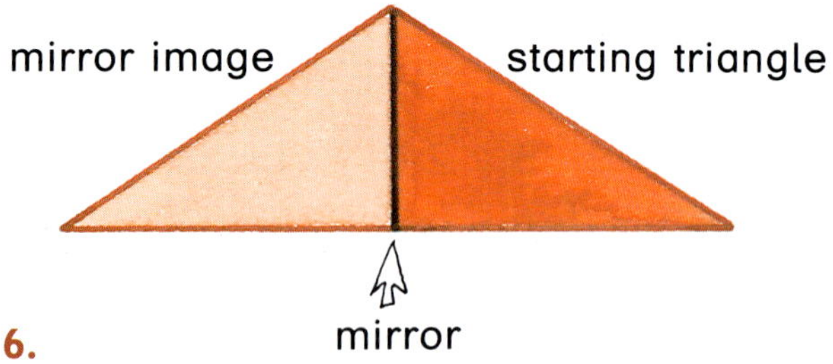

5.

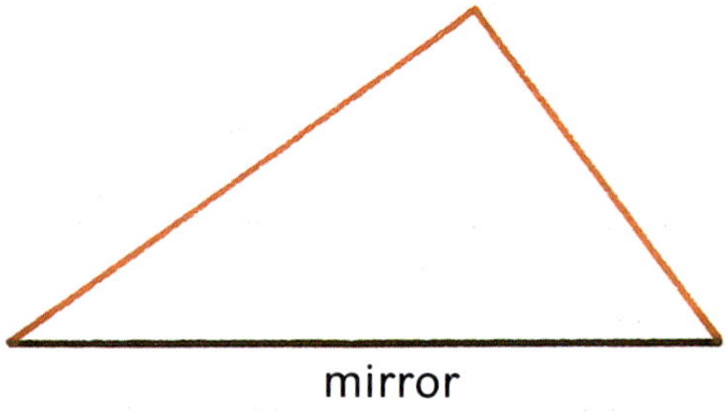

6.

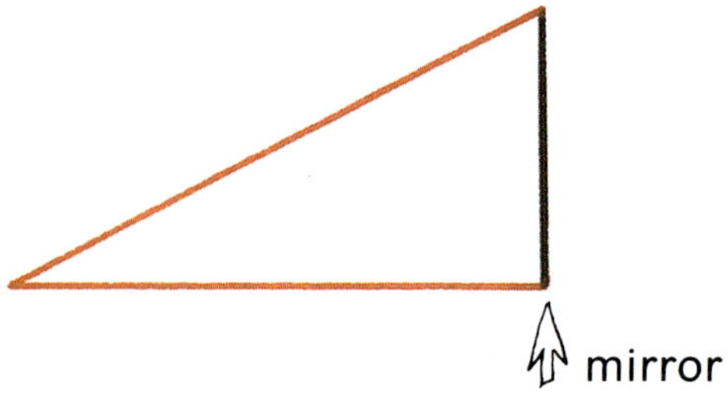

One perpendicular and the hypotenuse

You will need compasses, a set square, a ruler and paper.

If you know the lengths of one perpendicular and the hypotenuse of a right-angled triangle, you can draw it with compasses and a set square.

First draw the **perpendicular** (8 cm). Use the set-square to draw the **base** (quite long).

Set the compasses at 10 cm.

Put the point at the top of the **perpendicular** and make an arc which cuts the **base.**

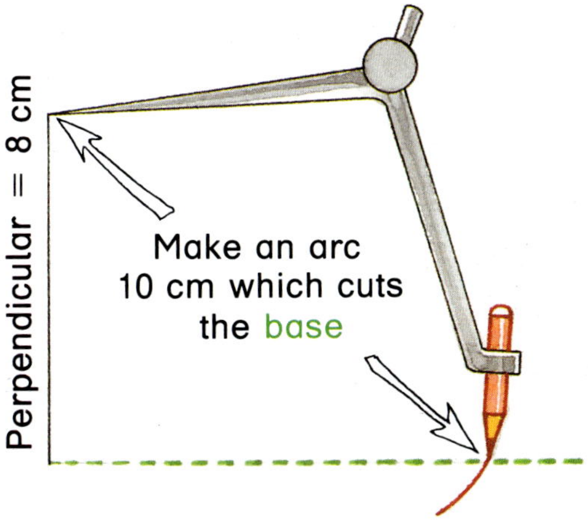

Use a set square to draw a base.

Draw the hypotenuse.

Draw these right-angled triangles. Write the length of the base.

1. hypotenuse 5 cm
   perpendicular 3 cm
2. hypotenuse 13 cm
   perpendicular 12 cm
3. hypotenuse 6.5 cm
   perpendicular 6 cm
4. hypotenuse 2.5 cm
   perpendicular 1.5 cm

Enlargements

Measure these right-angled triangles. Enlarge them by doubling the lengths of the sides.

5.

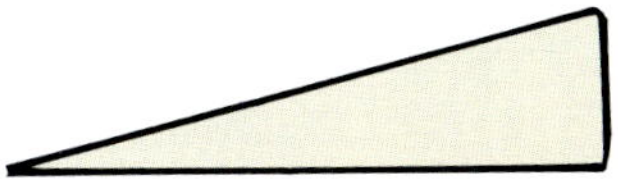

6.

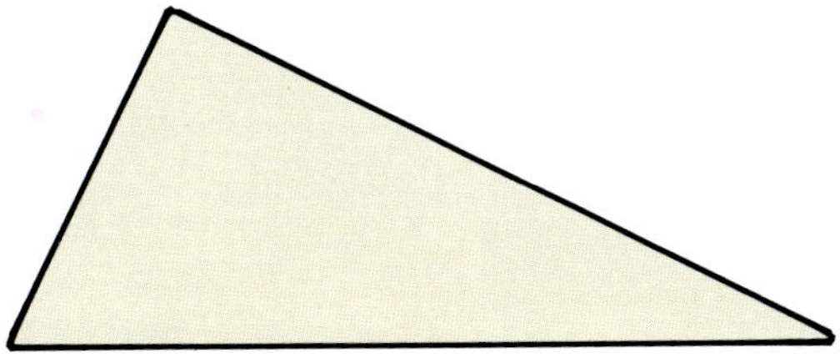

There is more about drawing triangles on page 94.

Matching shapes to their nets

Here are 5 solid shapes and 5 nets.

Which shape does each net make?

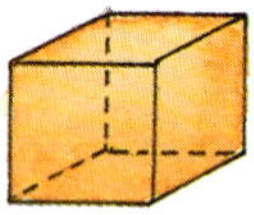
cube

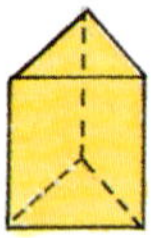
triangular prism

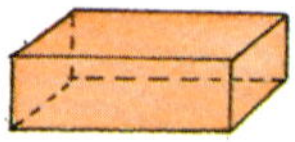
cuboid

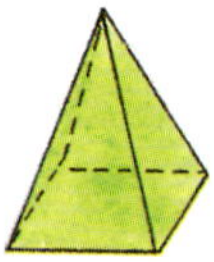
square pyramid

cylinder

1.

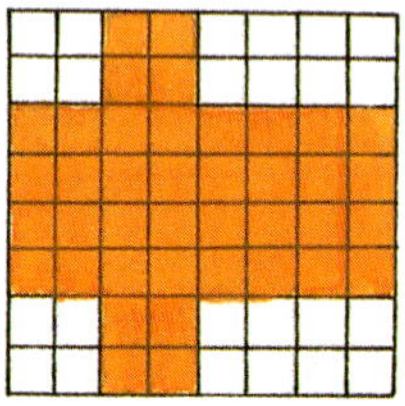

2.

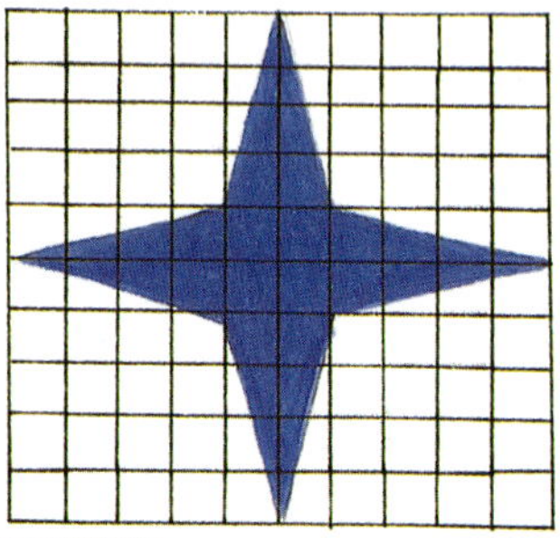

3.

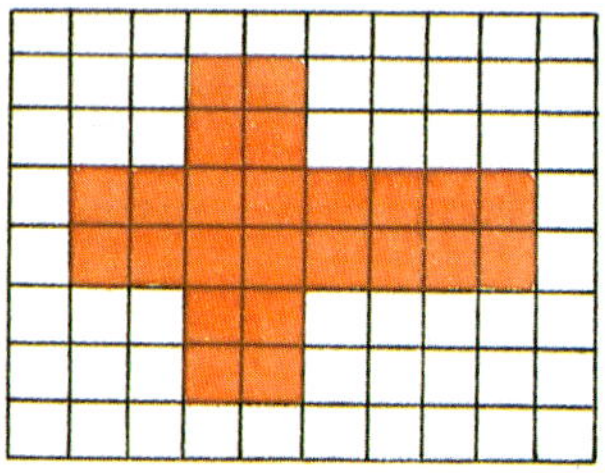

4.

5.

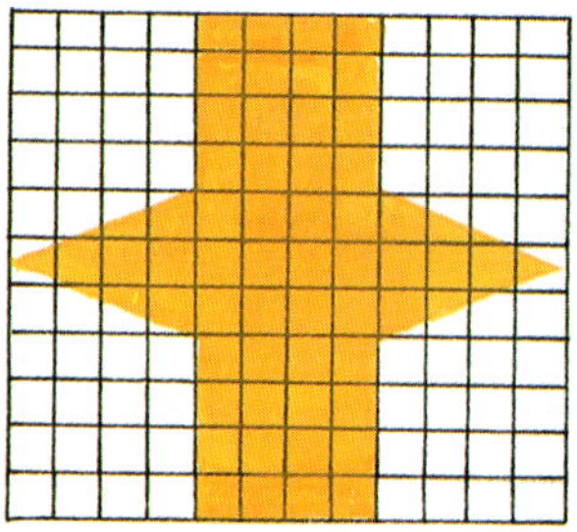

6. Which of these nets will make a cube?

a.

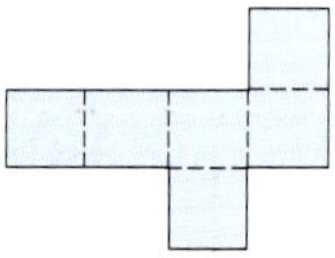

b.

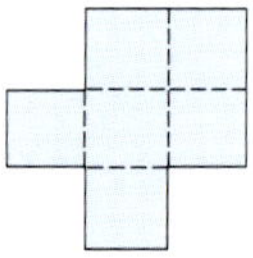

c.

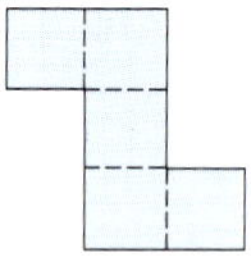

d.

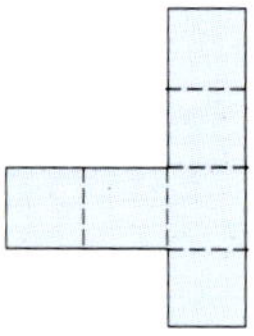

e.

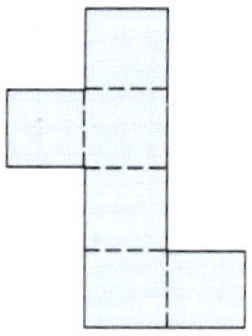

f.

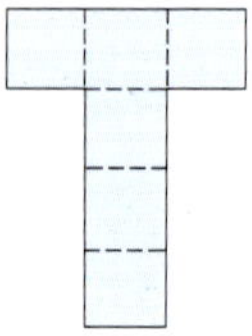

Investigating faces, edges and vertices

Remember: a face of a solid is a flat surface.

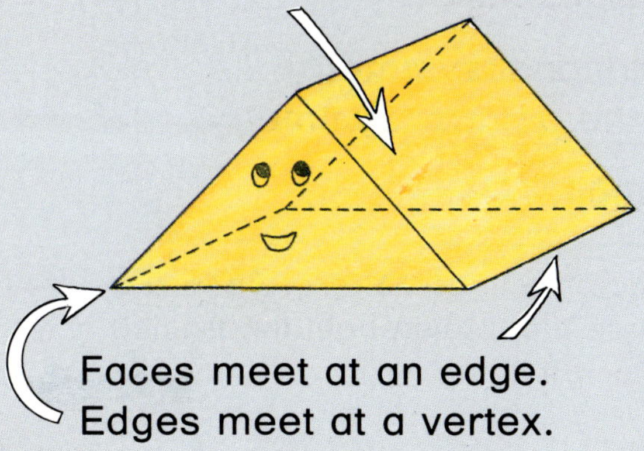

Faces meet at an edge.
Edges meet at a vertex.

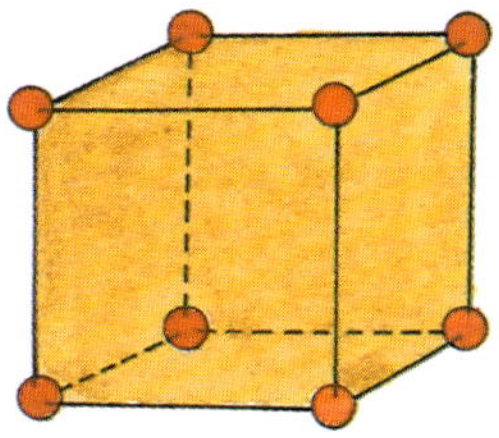

This cube has 6 faces

12 edges (black lines)

8 vertices (red dots)

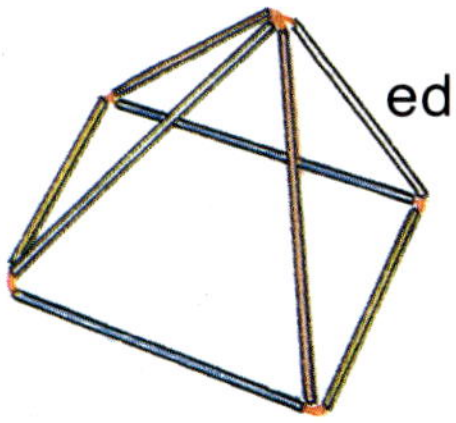

You can use straws and pipecleaners to make the edges and vertices of solid shapes.

1. Make these shapes using straws: cuboid; triangular prism; tetrahedron; square pyramid.
2. Count the faces, vertices and edges.
3. Make a chart like this. Try other solid shapes.
4. How could you find out the number of edges if you know how many faces and vertices?

Shape	Faces	Vertices	Edges
Cube	6	8	12
Cuboid			
Triangular prism			
Tetrahedron			
Square pyramid			

How many turns?

The flower below can be rotated about a point to a new position and appear identical.

The flower possesses rotational symmetry.
The centre of rotation is the point of symmetry.

Using tracing to find rotational symmetry.

Trace the figure. Press a pencil on the centre and rotate the tracing until the tracing and the original coincide again.

point of symmetry

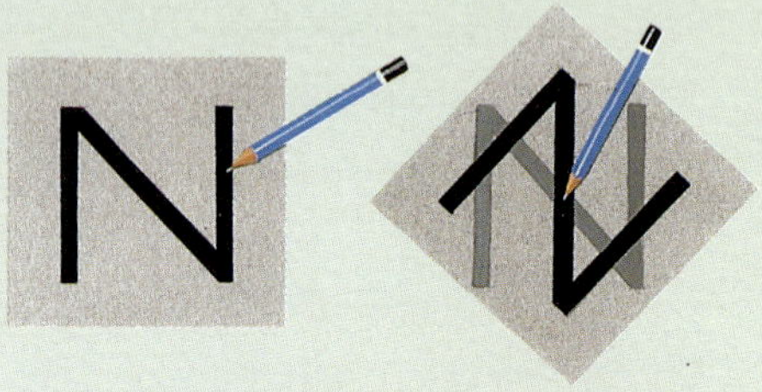

This tracing maps on to the original twice in a 360° turn. The order of rotational symmetry for N is 2.

If a shape can be rotated and fitted back in place three times, it has rotational symmetry order 3.
Four times, order 4, and so on.
Order 1 means no rotational symmetry.

Trace these letters. Write their order of symmetry.

1. B 2. H 3. I 4. K 5. O 6. T 7. X 8. Y 9. Z

Investigate these symbols in the same way.

capital letters of the Greek alphabet

Γ Δ Θ Λ Ξ
Π Σ Φ Ψ Ω

astronomy symbols

Rotational symmetry in everyday life

Here are some shapes and symbols you can see every day.

Trace them and show their lines of symmetry.

Write their order of rotational symmetry.

1.

2. 

3. 

4. 

5. 

6. 

7. 

8. 

9. 

Many crossword puzzles have rotational symmetry.

10. Copy this puzzle.

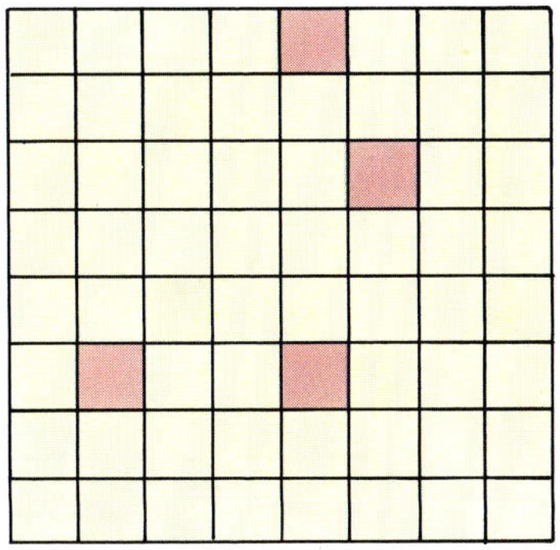

Shade in the least number of squares in order for the puzzle to have rotational symmetry of order 4.

11. Examine crossword puzzles in newspapers and magazines. Try to find three examples with rotational symmetry. Try to find a puzzle that does not have rotational symmetry. Try to find a puzzle that has line symmetry.

Ounces, pounds, stones, hundredweights and tons

In Britain, people used to measure all weights with these Imperial measures.

Ounces (oz)	There are 16 oz in 1 pound.
Pounds (lb)	There are 14 lbs in 1 stone.
Stones (st)	There are 8 st in 1 hundredweight.
Hundredweights (cwt)	There are 20 cwt in 1 ton.

Children used to have to convert from one weight to another. Try these for yourself.

1. How many ounces in 3 lbs?
2. How many pounds in 2 cwt?
3. How many stones in 5 cwt?
4. How many stones in $2\frac{1}{2}$ tons?
5. How many pounds in 1 ton?
6. How many ounces in 1 ton?

The coalman

The coalman used to deliver coal in 1 cwt sacks. He had to load his lorry every morning. The list shows his orders for Monday.

7. How many sacks did he need to load?
8. How much did his lorry carry on Monday?
9. On Tuesday, he carried 5 tons. How many sacks did he have to load?

Orders for Monday

8 cwt
5 cwt
1 ton
$\frac{1}{2}$ ton
15 cwt
7 cwt
12 cwt
2 cwt
5 cwt

Loose sweets

In many small sweetshops you can buy loose sweets from jars. They are sold in $\frac{1}{4}$lbs (quarter pounds).

What would these cost?

1. $\frac{1}{4}$lb of Sherbert Lemons and $\frac{1}{2}$lb of Winter Mixture.
2. $\frac{1}{2}$lb of Cola Fizz and $\frac{1}{4}$lb of Mixed Chocolates.
3. $\frac{1}{4}$lb each of Cough Candy, Winter Mixture and Sherbert Lemon.
4. 1 lb of Mixed Chocolates.
5. 2 lb of Cough Candy and $\frac{1}{4}$lb of Winter Mixture.
6. How much would your bag weigh if you bought $\frac{1}{2}$lb of each type of sweet?

Weigh yourself

Use old bathroom scales or the school's weighing machine.

7. Weigh yourself in stones and pounds.
8. Weigh yourself in kilograms and compare them with the stones and pounds.
9. Weigh some friends both ways. Make a chart.
10. Can you find a way to convert kilograms to stones and pounds?

Journey times

Use the railway timetable to answer these questions.

1. What time does the 08.06 from Hounslow reach Waterloo?
2. How long does it take the 09.04 from Hounslow to reach Putney?
3. You have to reach Clapham Junction at 4 o'clock in the afternoon. What is the latest train you could catch from Brentford?
4. What is the last train you could catch to Waterloo from Hounslow?
5. Which is the fastest train from Hounslow to Waterloo?
6. How long does it usually take to get from Syon Lane to Clapham Junction?
7. What time does the last train of the morning leave Barnes Bridge and arrive at Waterloo?
8. You arrive at Chiswick at 10 past 8 in the morning. What time is the next train you can catch to Waterloo?

HOUNSLOW - BARNES BRIDGE TO WATERLOO

Monday to Friday

	57	87	89	87	87 A	89 A	87 A	89 A	13 A
Hounslow ⊖ P	d 05 20	06 35	06 38	07 04	07 34	07 36	07 54	08 06	08 18
Isleworth	d 05 23	06 38	–	07 07	07 37	–	07 57	–	08 21
Syon Lane	d 05 25	06 40	–	07 09	07 39	–	07 59	–	–
Brentford	d 05 27	06 42	–	07 11	07 41	–	08 01	–	08 24
Kew Bridge	d 05 29	06 44	–	07 13	07 43	–	08 04	–	–
Chiswick	d 05 32	06 47	–	07 16	07 46	–	08 06	–	–
Barnes Bridge	d 05 34	06 49	–	07 18	07 48	–	08 09	–	–
Barnes P.	d 05 36	06 52	06 58	07 20	07 50	–	08 11	–	08 31
Putney	d 05 39	06 55	07 01	07 23	07 53	07 59	08 13	08 28	08 33
Wandsworth Town	d 05 41	06 57	07 03	07 25	07 55	–	–	–	–
Clapham Junction	d 05 43	06 59	07 05	07 27	07 58	08 04	08 18	08 33	08 38
Queenstown Road (Batt)	d 05 46	07 02	07 08	07 30	08 01	–	–	–	08 41
Vauxhall ⊖	d 05 49	07 05	07 11	07 33	08 04	08 10	08 23	08 41	08 44
London Waterloo ⊖	a 05 53	07 11	07 17	07 39	08 10	08 16	08 29	08 47	08 50

Monday to Friday *continued*

	37 1 A	87 A	89 A	13 A	89 A	13	13
Hounslow ⊖ P	d 08 29	08 35	08 38	09 01	09 04	09 31	10 01
Isleworth	d –	08 38	–	09 04	–	09 34	10 04
Syon Lane	d –	08 40	–	09 06	–	09 36	10 06
Brentford	d –	08 42	–	09 08	–	09 38	10 08
Kew Bridge	d –	08 45	–	09 10	–	09 40	10 10
Chiswick	d –	08 47	–	09 13	–	09 43	10 13
Barnes Bridge	d –	08 50	–	09 15	–	09 45	10 15
Barnes P.	d –	08 54	–	09 19	09 23	09 48	10 18
Putney	d –	08 57	09 00	09 21	09 25	09 50	10 20
Wandsworth Town	d –	08 59	–	09 24	09 28	09 53	10 23
Clapham Junction	d 08 42	09 02	09 05	09 26	09 30	09 55	10 25
Queenstown Road (Batt)	d –	–	–	09 29	09 36	09 58	10 28
Vauxhall ⊖	d –	09 07	09 11	09 32	09 39	10 01	10 31
London Waterloo ⊖	a 08 53	09 13	09 17	09 38	09 45	10 05	10 35

Monday to Friday *continued*

	13		87	13	13	89	13	87
Hounslow ⊖ P	d 10 31		15 01	15 31	16 09	16 22	16 31	17 12
Isleworth	d 10 34		15 04	15 34	16 12	–	16 34	17 15
Syon Lane	d 10 36		15 06	15 36	16 14	–	16 36	17 17
Brentford	d 10 38		15 08	15 38	16 16	–	16 38	17 19
Kew Bridge	3 10 40		15 10	15 40	16 18	–	16 40	17 21
Chiswick	d 10 43	and every 30	15 13	15 43	16 21	–	16 43	17 24
Barnes Bridge	d 10 45	minutes until	15 15	15 45	16 23	–	16 45	17 26
Barnes P.	d 10 48		15 18	15 48	16 28	16 40	16 48	17 30
Putney	d 10 50		15 20	15 50	16 31	16 43	16 50	17 33
Wandsworth Town	d 10 53		15 23	15 53	16 33	16 45	16 53	17 35
Clapham Junction	d 10 55		15 25	15 55	16 35	16 47	16 55	17 37
Queenstown Road (Batt)	d 10 58		15 28	15 58	16 38	16 50	16 58	17 40
Vauxhall ⊖	d 11 01		15 31	16 01	16 41	16 53	17 01	17 43
London Waterloo ⊖	a 11 05		15 35	16 05	16 45	16 58	17 05	17 48

Monday to Friday *continued*

	89	87	87	89	87	87	13	13	13
Hounslow ⊖ P	d 1709	17 42	18 12	18 09	18 42	19 05	19 31	20 02	20 31
Isleworth	d –	17 45	18 15	–	18 45	19 08	19 34	20 05	20 34
Syon Lane	d –	17 47	18 17	–	18 47	19 10	19 36	20 07	20 36
Brentford	d –	17 49	18 19	–	18 49	19 12	19 38	20 09	20 38
Kew Bridge	d –	17 51	18 21	–	18 51	19 14	19 40	20 11	20 40
Chiswick	d –	17 54	18 24	–	18 54	19 17	19 43	20 14	20 43
Barnes Bridge	d –	17 56	18 26	–	18 56	19 19	19 45	20 16	20 45
Barnes P.	d 17 33	18 00	18 30	18 33	18 59	19 21	19 48	20 18	20 48
Putney	d 17 36	18 03	18 33	18 35	19 01	19 24	19 50	20 21	20 50
Wandsworth Town	d 17 38	18 05	18 35	18 38	19 04	19 26	19 53	20 23	20 53
Clapham Junction	d 17 40	18 07	18 37	18 40	19 06	19 28	19 55	20 25	20 55
Queenstown Road (Batt)	d 17 43	18 10	18 40	18 43	19 09	19 31	19 58	20 28	20 58
Vauxhall ⊖	d 17 46	18 13	18 43	18 46	19 12	19 34	20 01	20 31	21 01
London Waterloo ⊖	d 17 52	18 17	18 47	18 52	19 18	19 38	20 05	20 35	21 05

Set your video

To set a video recorder you need to tell it the starting and finishing times of the programme you want to record. You have to use 24-hour time

For example, CHILDREN'S BBC begins at 4.10 in the afternoon. This is 16:10 in 24-hour time

BBC

4.10 CHILDREN'S BBC: Babar. *2163869* 4.35 **Uncle Jack and Operation Green.** *5216753* 5.0 **Newsround.** *2014937* 5.5 **Record Breakers.** *1364537* The re-run of the 20th anniversary series sees Roy Castle chatting to Helen Sharman, Britain's first female space traveller. Plus a report on Status Quo's rock 'n' marathon concert tour. (S)(T)

5.35 NEIGHBOURS. *734376* Joe takes cover at Doug's, hoping to escape from the threats, but before long there's another menacing call. Todd and Cody receive their punishment for going to the nightclub – they're banned from seeing each other. The rows between Paul and Jim reach fever pitch. (R)(S)(T)

6.0 NEWS; Weather. *27* (T)

6.30 REGIONAL NEWS MAGAZINE. *79*

7.0 TOP OF THE POPS. *6111* Tony Dortie sorts out the chart hits and new releases. (S)

7.30 EASTENDERS. *63* That sensitive diplomat Pete takes it upon himself to have a confidential word in pushy Mrs Hewitt's ear. His aim, of course, is to stop the gossip about her and Arthur spreading beyond the 16 million or so who are already full of it. The result may be rather different. Mandy's still looking for a job and wondering if Ian – famous for his social conscience – might help. (S)(T)

8.0 EVERY SECOND COUNTS. *2531* Three more couples take deep breaths and plunge into Paul Daniel's quick-fire quiz game. (S)

8.30 RUSS ABBOT. *1666* What a cast! Cooperman, Dr Spook, Barratt Holmes and Heinz von Meatball. And all down to Russ. There's a way to save money. Les Dennis, Jeffrey Holland and Sherrie Hewson are among the extras. (R)(S)(T)

9.0 NEWS (T)**; Regional News; Weather.** *1260*

ITV

3.55 CHILDREN'S ITV: Huxley Pig. *1504647* (R) 4.5 **T-Bag and the Pearls of Wisdom.** *6501376* (R) 4.30 **Rolf's Cartoon Club.** *42* (R) 5.0 **Cartoon.** *9078598* 5.10 **Who's the Boss?** *6861774* Angela's fed up with her lifestyle.

5.40 NEWS (T)**; Weather**. *905937*

5.55 THAMES HELP. *220024* (R)

6.0 HOME AND AWAY. *95* Finlay reckons she's going to give up her education. Adam launches himself into a new business venture. (R)(T)

6.30 THAMES NEWS. *47* (T)

7.0 EMMERDALE. *8579* Suddenly the sun is shining. Wedding bells are being booked and even Mark has brighter hopes about his future. But, soaps being what they are, there is always a dark cloud on the horizon and it looms for Nick as a knock on his door leads to a nightmare. (T)

7.30 THE FULL TREATMENT. *31* Ten per cent of British people suffer from migraines, losing some £300 million a year in working days. Here's news that attacks can be halved by recognising and avoiding certain 'trigger' factors. Plus ideas for helping stroke survivors and children who suffer severe brain damage from cerebral palsy. (R)

8.0 THE BILL. *7227* On his last day at Sun Hill, Dashwood collects his leaving present, chosen by Burnside, no less, and counts on some easy farewell hours. One way and another his goodbye shift is one he would have preferred to have missed. (T)

8.30 THIS WEEK. *6734* In-depth analysis of an issue of current concern. (T)

9.0 LA LAW. *5579* A *Dallas*-type surprise for Markowitz as, out of the blue, he discovers he has a 16-year-old daughter from a previous and, presumably, long-forgotten relationship. (S)(T)

Write the times you would set your video to record these programmes. Remember you need a start time and a finish time for each programme.

1. Neighbours followed by Home and Away.
2. Record Breakers followed by Emmerdale.
3. Huxley Pig followed by Russ Abbot.
4. Top of the Pops, followed by The Bill, followed by LA Law.
5. Write the times to set a video recorder for your favourite programmes from the list.

How many rectangles?

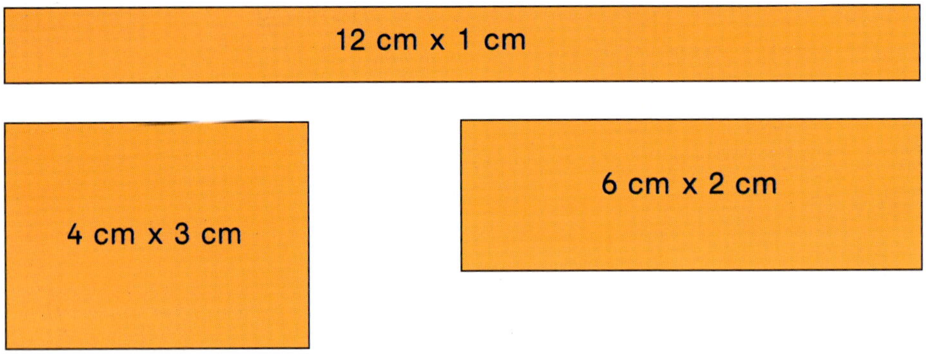

All of these rectangles have an area of 12 cm^2, but different lengths and breadths.

Write down all the possible lengths and breadths of rectangles and squares with these areas.
You may wish to draw them on squared paper.

1. 8 cm^2 **2.** 16 cm^2 **3.** 24 cm^2

4. 18 cm^2 **5.** 36 cm^2 **6.** 20 cm^2

Series of rectangles

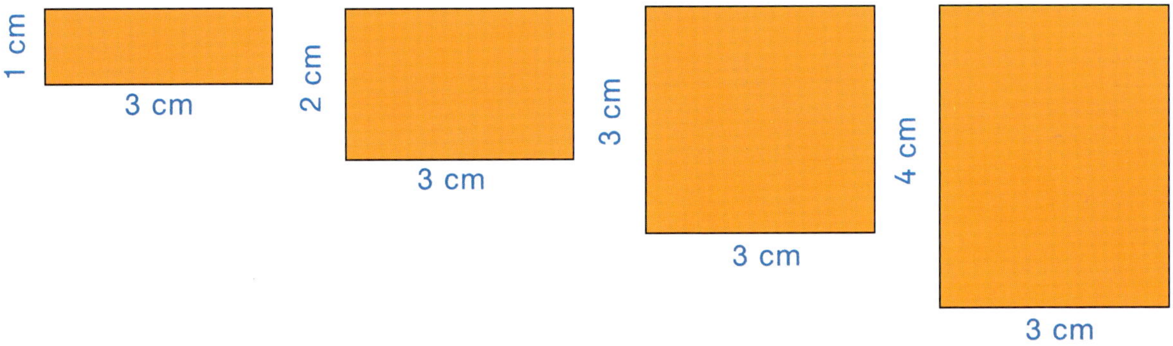

7. In this series, one side increases in length by 1 cm each time.

Make a chart like this one and continue the series.

Describe any patterns you find.

length	*breadth*	*area*

Double the dimensions

Remember: the dimensions of a shape are its measurements.

Draw each of these shapes on centimetre squared paper. Write their areas.

Double the dimensions of each shape and draw the larger shapes. Write down the new areas. Write what you notice about the change in area.

1.

2.

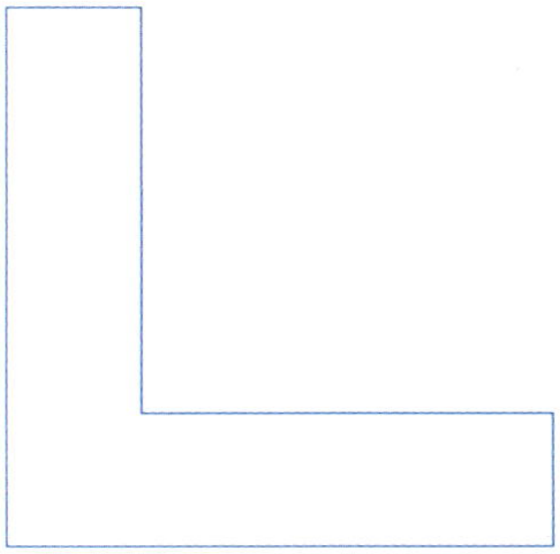

3.

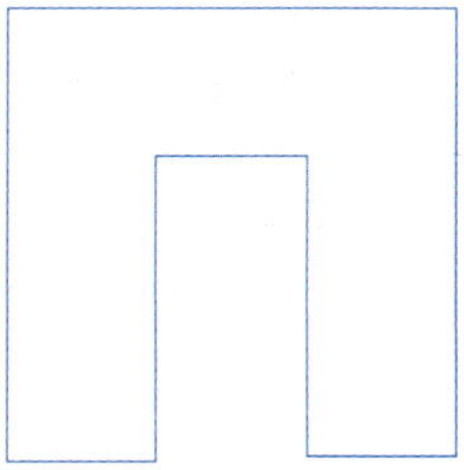

4.

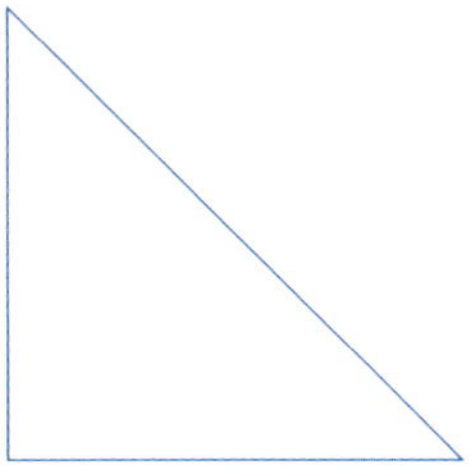

5.

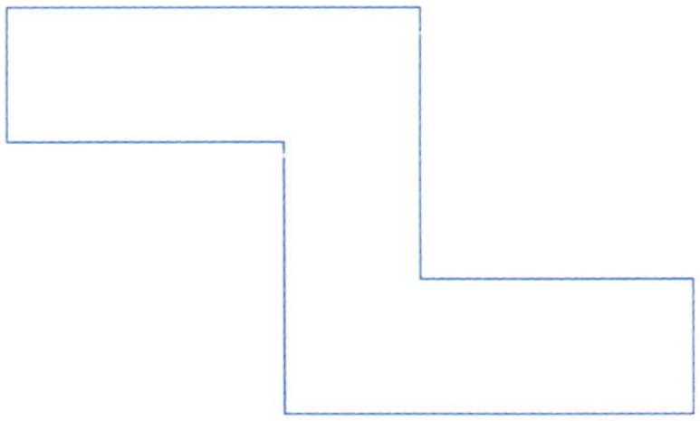

6.

7.

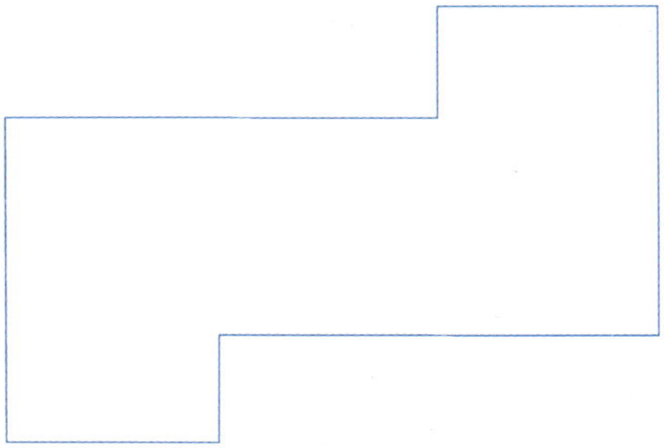

Decision trees

You can use a decision tree to sort and identify things.

The questions in the boxes will separate the items so that there is only **one** at the very end of each branch.

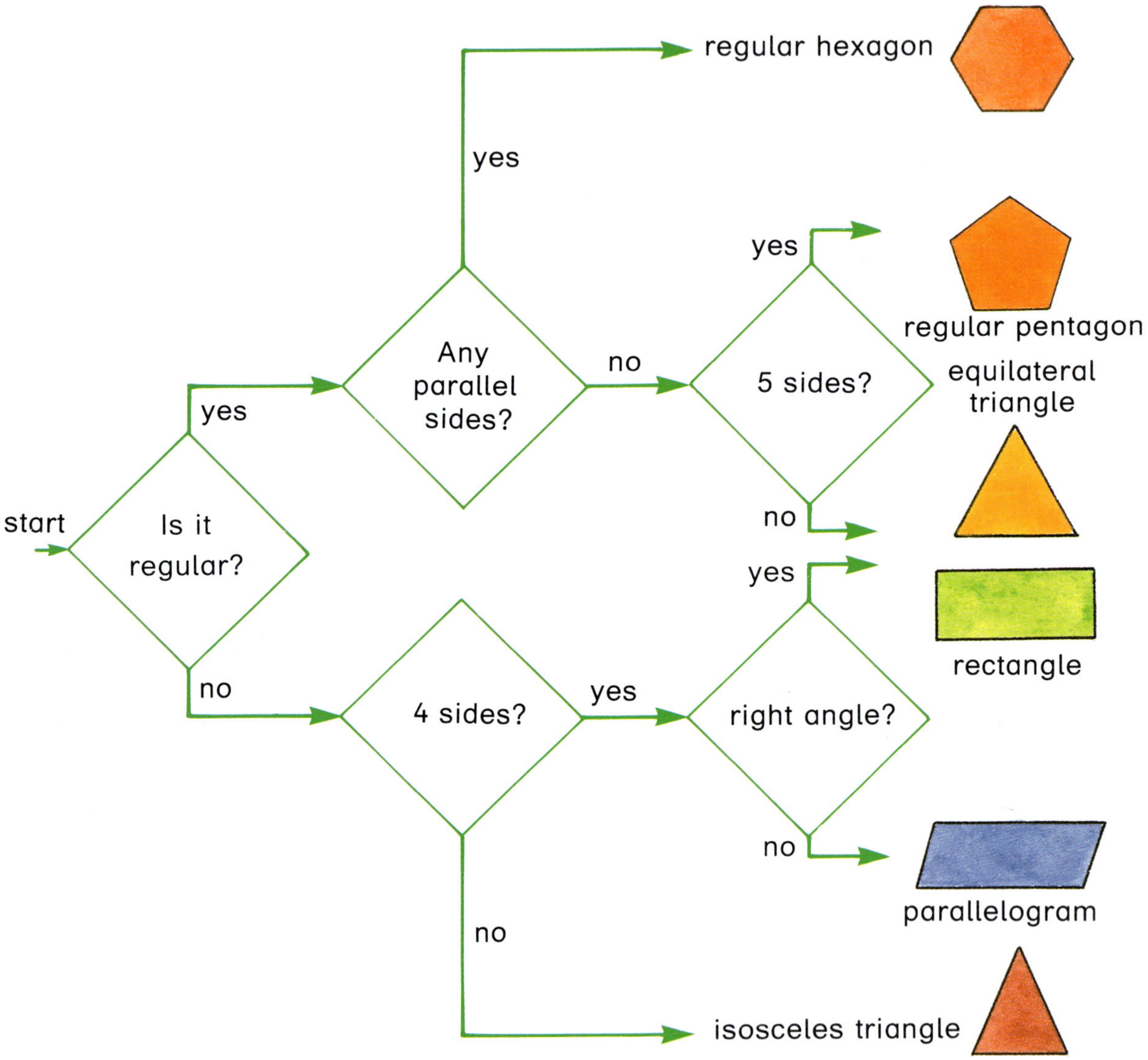

This is a decision tree for sorting shapes.

There are some questions about it on the next page.

What is the shape?

Use the decision tree on page 66 to answer these questions.

1. Which shape is regular, with 5 sides, but no sides parallel?
2. Which shape is not regular and does not have 4 sides?
3. Which shape is regular, with fewer than 5 sides and no parallel sides?
4. Which shape is irregular, with 4 sides and no right angles?
5. Which shape is regular, with some parallel sides?
6. Which shapes are irregular with 4 sides?

Fishy facts

Make your own decision tree to sort the fish from this database.

Name	lives in:	eats:	shape:	markings:
blue shark	sea	other fish	streamlined	none
plaice	sea	sand worms	flat	red spots
pike	fresh water	other fish	streamlined	yellow spots
perch	fresh water	other fish	rounded	stripes
brown trout	fresh water	insects	streamlined	brown spots

There is more about decision trees on page 99.

Test scores

Name	Reading Age	Maths Score
Panthratan	9.8	62
Tony	11.7	73
Mustafa	10.5	65
Katriona	7.5	54
Amardeep	12.8	79
Krunal	10.7	81
Graham	11.2	68
Dean	5.6	32
Inderjeet	10.5	75
Harpreet	11.1	82
Lisa	8.7	61
Jaimeet	12.5	92
Jamie	10.7	74
Nichola	11.3	55
Christina	9.5	48
Rachael	13.4	89
Carl	10.7	83
Cherie	9.4	74
Scott	6.3	42
Siobhon	10.8	75
Rajesh	12.1	97
Vicky	8.6	65
Cheryl	11.7	78
Sandeep	10.9	71
Victoria	10.6	67
Paul	11.3	84
William	13.2	96
Khurram	9.7	77
Imran	10.9	82
Charlotte	12.3	91

Showing test scores

The database on page 68 shows the test results for a class.

1. Make a frequency table for the reading age scores. Use the ranges 5.0 to 5.9, 6.0 to 6.9, 7.0 to 7.9, and so on.
2. Draw a frequency diagram to show how many children were in each range.
3. Which range has most children?
4. Which range has fewest children?
5. Make a frequency table of the maths scores. Choose sensible ranges.
6. Draw a frequency diagram to show how many children were in each range.
7. Which range has most children?
8. Which range has fewest children?
9. Make up your own tables or spelling test for an imaginary class.

Draw a frequency table and frequency diagram to show the scores. Choose your own ranges.

Test your eyesight

1. Use this chart to test your eyesight.

   Ask a friend to hold it up for you.

   Walk back until you can no longer read the bottom line, the next line up, and so on.

   Keep a record of the distances and compare them with your friends.

   H A R

   F T E L

   O V N Q P

   X S B Z C I D

2. Make an eyesight chart for someone who cannot read letters of the alphabet, for example, for a small child, and try it out.

Find out more about yourself

Here are some unusual and interesting comparisons and problems to try.

1\.

If you were able to make a stack of £1 coins as tall as you are, how much money would there be?

2\.

Did you know that 80% of your body weight is water?

Approximately how many bucketfuls would that be?

3\.

How long is your hair?

How long is your best friend's hair?

What is the difference in length?

Who has the longest hair in the class?

Draw a diagram to show the length of everyone's hair.

4\.

Measure the circumference of your wrist.

Measure the circumference of your ankle.

Use a calculator to divide your wrist measurement by your ankle measurement.

Try the same with some friends and compare the results.

Are they similar?

Elephant house sums

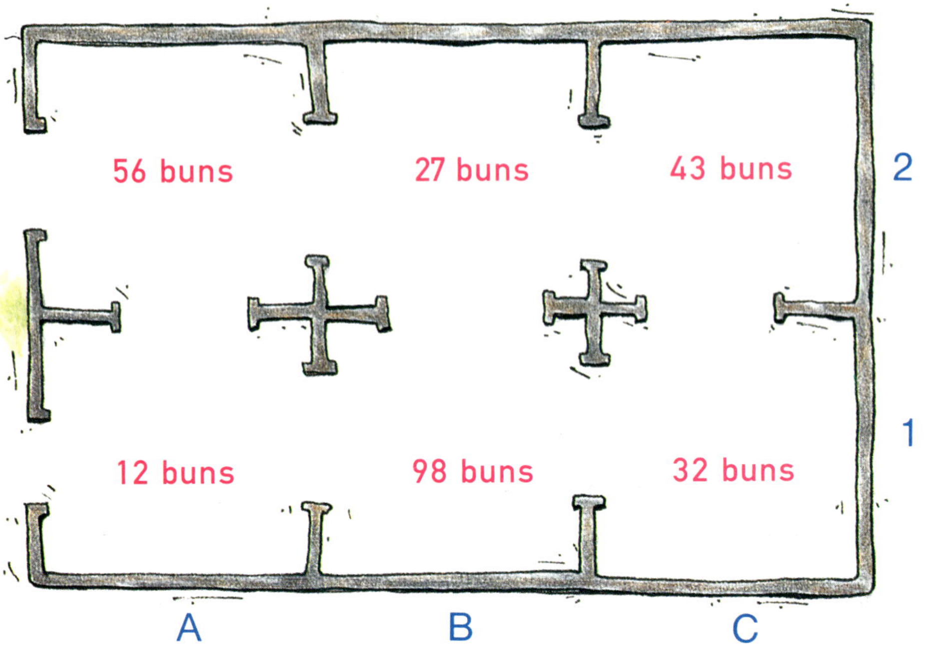

The elephant's keeper puts different numbers of buns in each room of the elephant house.

Answer these questions.

1. If the elephant went from A2 to A1 and B1 how many buns could he eat?

How many buns for these routes?

2. A1, B1, C1
3. A2, B2, C2
4. A1, B1, B2, C2
5. A2, B2, B1, C1
6. If the elephant was only allowed to eat buns in 3 rooms, which 3 rooms would give him the most buns? How many could he eat?

Draw your own elephant house with 8 rooms.

Put in some numbers.
Make up some problems.

Magic squares

2	7	6	→ 15
9	5	1	→ 15
4	3	8	→ 15

↙ 15 ↓ 15 ↓ 15 ↓ 15 ↘ 15

In a magic square each row, column and diagonal has the same sum.

Copy and complete each magic square.

1.

	2	
14	10	
4	18	8

2.

	30	
	50	
	70	20

3.

39		
43	38	
		37

4.

12	27	6
24	3	

5.

		100
	125	225
		50

6. Choose any magic square.

Multiply each number by 2.

Do you still have a magic square?

---

7. Subtraction and addition investigation

Take a 3-digit number.	734
Reverse it,	437
take away,	297
reverse it,	792
add.	1089

Try a different 3-digit number and do the same.

What answer do you get?

Does it always work?

Try it with 2-digit numbers.

Try it with 4-digit numbers.

Find all the factors

1. Write all the numbers to 20 as a list like this one.

   For each number find all its factors and write them alongside it.

   Count up the factors for each number and write the total.

Number	Factors	Number of Factors
1	1	1
2	1, 2	2
3	1, 3	2
4	1, 2, 4	3
5	1, 5	2
6		

Answer these questions.

2. Which numbers have only two factors?
3. What is the largest number of factors?
4. What sort of numbers have an odd number of factors?
5. What is the most common number of factors?
6. What is the least common number of factors?
7. Now investigate all the numbers from 21 to 40 in the same way.

Missing numbers

The rain has smudged out some of the numbers on Paul's homework. Help him by writing it all out correctly.

They are all multiplications and divisions.

1. 4 x 3 = 123	**2.** 84 ÷ = 12
3. 19 x 6 =	**4.** 48 ÷ = 8
5. x 4 = 140	**6.** 56 ÷ = 8
7. 63 ÷ = 7	**8.** 27 = 81
9. 72 = 9	**10.** 42 = 168

Highest factors

24 has the factors 1, 2, 3, 4, 6, **8**, 12, 24

64 has the factors 1, 2, 4, **8**, 16, 32, 64

The highest factor that they **both** have is 8.

Find the highest number that is a factor of each of these numbers.

11. 25, 40

12. 18, 45

13. 24, 36

14. 17, 31

15. 26, 52

16. 28, 42

Millions

After 999 999 comes 1 000 000 (one million).

after 1 000 000 comes 1 000 001 (one million and one).

Write these numbers using numerals.

1. Three million, five hundred thousand three hundred and fifty.
2. Eight million, nine hundred thousand.
3. Twelve million, two hundred thousand, eight hundred.
4. One hundred and twenty million, six hundred thousand four hundred and ninety-nine.

Write these numbers in words.

5. 5 650 000
6. 10 100 500
7. 25 000 000
8. 250 000 000

Collect the phone numbers of five or six friends. Write the numerals as millions or hundreds of thousands. Put them in order from the largest to the smallest.

What's the value?

25 987 654

The numeral 2 in this number is worth 20 million (20 000 000).

Write what the red numerals are worth in these numbers.

1. 7 854 962
2. 7 854 962
3. 15 750 500
4. 15 750 500
5. 125 340 750
6. 125 340 750
7. 55 946 675
8. 55 946 675

---

9. **Doubling up**

A grain of rice is placed in the first square of this grid.

Two grains are placed in the second square, four grains in the next, eight grains in the next, and so on.

Each time the number of grains is doubled.

Carry on doubling. How many grains will there be in the final square?

A calculator might be useful!

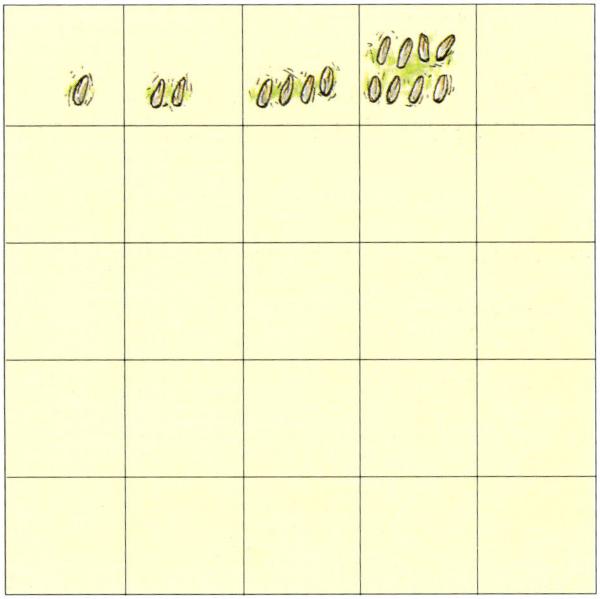

Magic squares

In a magic square the numbers in each row, each column and each diagonal add to the same answer.

Complete these magic squares. Only use a calculator to check your answers.

1.

	0.91	
1.17	0.65	0.13
		1.04

2.

0.78		
	1.95	
	1.17	3.12

3.

0.85	1.15	0.2	0.5	
1.2	0.25	0.3		
0.05	0.35	0.65		1.25
0.4	0.7		1.05	
0.75		1.1		

4. Make your own magic square.
Draw 9 squares in a 3 x 3 square.
Put in numbers with 2 decimal places to make a magic square. The numbers in questions 1 and 2 may help.

Gymnastics

Vault

Bars

Floor

Beam

There are four main events in this gymnastics competition.

Here are the scores of five competitors.

	Vault	Bars	Beam	Floor
Francesca	8.50	7.65	7.15	8.00
Barbara	7.85	8.35	7.40	8.25
Mina	8.25	7.80	8.20	8.50
Denise	8.10	8.55	8.80	9.10
Olga	7.95	8.25	8.5	8.75

To find the winner each person's four scores are added.

1. What is the total score for each competitor?

2. Write the total scores in order from greatest to least.

3. Write the names of the winners of the gold, silver and bronze medals.

What was the question?

4. John ended up with 13.25 in his calculator display.

   Write down two additions and two subtractions he might have used to get this answer.

There is more about adding and subtracting decimals on page 82.

Decimals on your calculator

Add or subtract to get the number in the display.

Use only the keys shown.

You may use the keys more than once.

Write a number sentence for each one.

1. 

2. 

3. 

4. 

5. 

6. 

7. 

8. 

9. **What was the question?**

Menisha ended up with 125.75 in her calculator display.

Write down any five questions she might have used to get this answer.

Change the display

42.73 Chi Wing started with this number in his calculator.

He wanted to change it to 15.5 .

He wrote down the steps he took.

42.73 → (−20) → 22.73 → (−7) → 15.73 → (−0.03) → 15.7 → (−0.2) → 15.5

Write the steps you take to change these numbers.

1. 25.34 ⟶ 5.2
2. 16.25 ⟶ 50.75
3. 48.3 ⟶ 10.55
4. 16.5 ⟶ 8.25
5. 29.75 ⟶ 58.25
6. 17.35 ⟶ 34.7

7. **Shortest steps game** (for 2 or more people)

You will need a counter, a calculator for each player, 2 sets of cards with the numerals 0 to 9 on them.

Spread the cards out face down. Turn over three cards.

Use the counter to make a decimal number.

3 ● 6 1 Put the number into your calculators.

Re-arrange the cards and counter to make a new number 1 6 ● 3

The person to change the display to the new number in the **fewest steps** wins.

Bills, bills and more bills

Sometimes people make mistakes when working out bills.

Quantity	Item	Price of each	Cost
5	pencils	£0.29	£1.45
2	pads of paper	£1.89	£3.87
2	notebooks	£3.25	£3.25
8	bookcovers	£0.35	£2.40
3	ballpoint pens	£0.69	£1.38
		Total	£12.45

1. Write out this bill again, putting all the mistakes right.
2. What is the difference between the old total and the correct total?

The Sports Wear Shop had a sale.
Find the total bill for each of these customers.

3. Name Ravinder

Article	Number bought	Price for 1	Cost X
track trousers	1		
T-shirts	3		
socks	2 pr		
running shoes	1 pr		
	Total +		

4. Name Lesley

Article	Number bought	Price for 1	Cost X
T-shirts	2		
socks	3 pr		
shorts	1		
track trousers	2		
jacket	1		
	Total +		

How much shopping do they carry?

These are the weights of tins, jars and packets in the supermarket.

Tin of soup	0.43kg
Baked Beans	0.45kg
Tin of Corned Beef	0.20kg
Tin of Tomatoes	0.39kg
Tin of Sardines	0.12kg
Tin of Salmon	0.21kg
Cat Food	0.40kg
Jar of Jam	0.45kg
Jar of Peanut Butter	0.22kg
Jar of Pickles	0.33kg
Muesli	0.75kg
Bran Flakes	0.50kg
Weetabix	0.84kg
Loaf	0.55kg

How much does each person's shopping weigh?

1. Mr Lee buys,
   2 tins of cat food, 2 tins of soup, 1 loaf, 1 tin of beans.
2. Mrs Hobbs buys,
   1 tin of corned beef, 2 tins of tomatoes, 1 tin of salmon, 2 jars of jam, 2 loaves.
3. Mrs Walsh buys,
   Bran Flakes, Weetabix, 1 jar of peanut butter, 1 loaf, 1 tin of corned beef, Muesli, 1 jar of pickles.
4. If you bought one of everything, how much would it weigh?

Missing decimal points

In these sentences the decimal points have been left out. Write them **with** the decimal points so that they make sense.

5. 365 metres of carpet are joined to 150 metres of carpet. The whole carpet is now 515 metres long.
6. 45 litres of paint will be needed to decorate downstairs. 275 litres will be needed for upstairs. We will need 725 litres altogether.

Percentages

Per cent means for each hundred.
The symbol % means per cent.

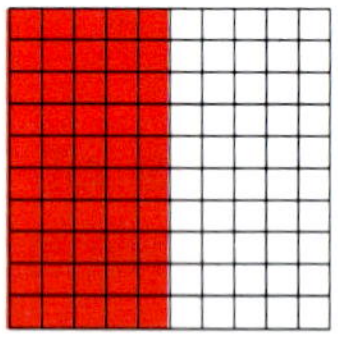

50% (or $\frac{1}{2}$) of this 100 square is coloured red.

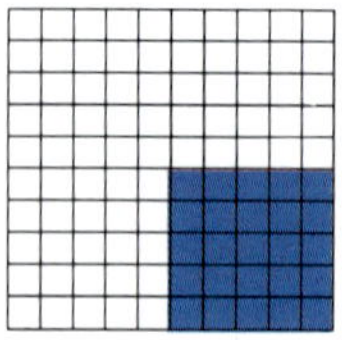

25% (or $\frac{1}{4}$) of this 100 square is coloured blue.

What percentage of these squares is coloured?

1. 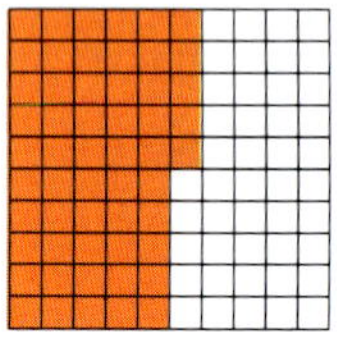

2. 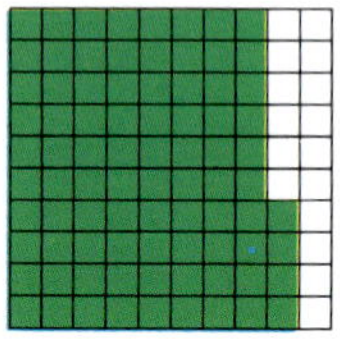

3. 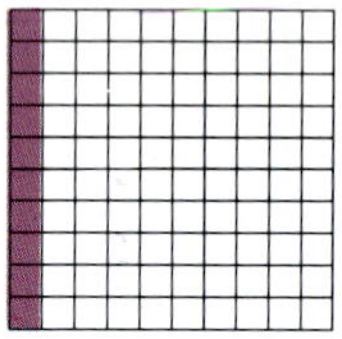

4. 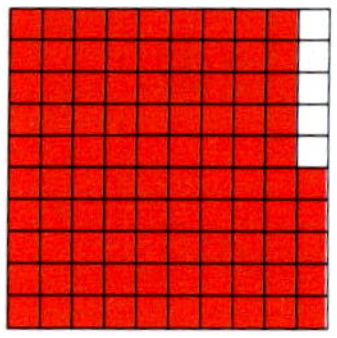

5. 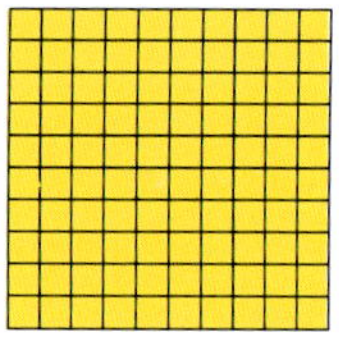

6. 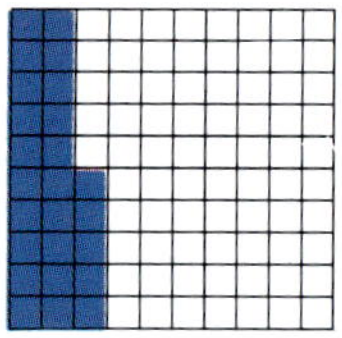

Use 100 squares and colour these percentages.

7. 33%

8. 15%

9. 75%

Answer these questions.

10. Richard got 86 out of 100 questions correct. What percentage did he score?

11. A package of 100 marbles contains 50 red marbles and 30 blue ones.

What percentage of the marbles is red?

What percentage of the marbles is blue?

What percentage of the marbles is neither red nor blue?

12. Jenny has 100 stamps in her album. 63 stamps are Canadian. What percentage is not Canadian?

Discounts

Remember:

10% means

10 out of every 100

OR

one tenth $\frac{1}{10}$

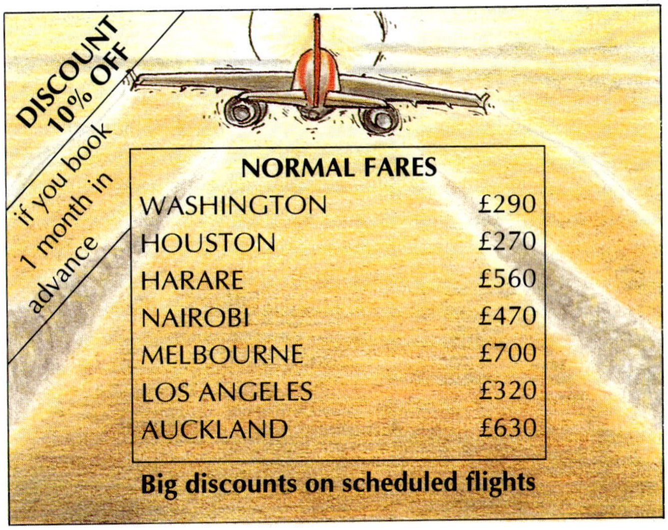

Write the fares to these cities if you book 1 month in advance

1. Los Angeles **2.** Nairobi **3.** Auckland

4. Harare **5.** Houston **6.** Washington

This is a symmetrical pattern on 100 squares.

What percentage is:

7. red

8. yellow

9. blue

10. green

11. Make your own symmetrical pattern on 100 squares. Write the percentages of the colours you use.

There is more about percentages on page 86.

Planning a garden

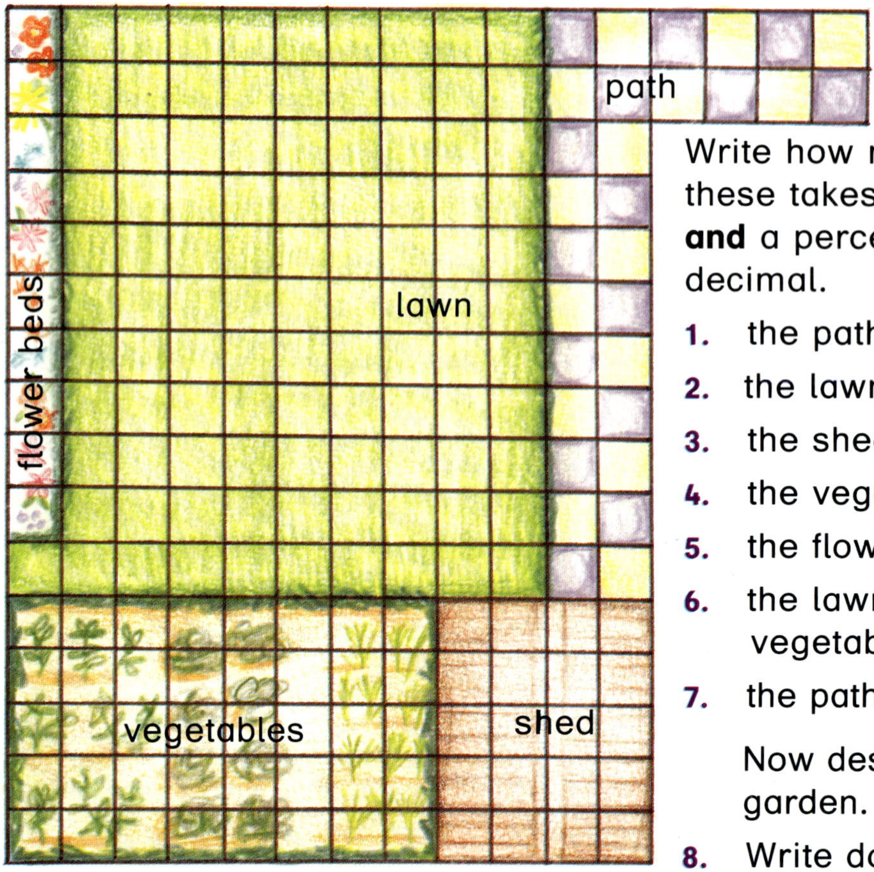

This plan of a garden has 200 squares.

Write how much each of these takes up as a fraction **and** a percentage **and** a decimal.

1. the path
2. the lawn
3. the shed
4. the vegetable patch
5. the flower beds
6. the lawn and the vegetable patch
7. the path and flower beds

Now design your own garden.

8. Write down the fraction, percentage and decimal for each area.

$\frac{1}{2}$	0.6	40%	0.75	50%	$\frac{1}{4}$	$\frac{3}{6}$
$\frac{6}{10}$	$\frac{3}{4}$	0.5	$\frac{2}{8}$	60%	$\frac{4}{10}$	75%
$\frac{2}{5}$	25%	35%	$\frac{5}{10}$	0.4	$\frac{3}{5}$	0.25

9. Write down the sets of cards which show the same amounts. For example, $\frac{1}{2}$, 50%, and so on.

10. Which card is the odd one out?

Fractions, decimals and percentages

In a survey, people were asked what kind of TV programme they liked. The answers were shown on a chart of percentages.

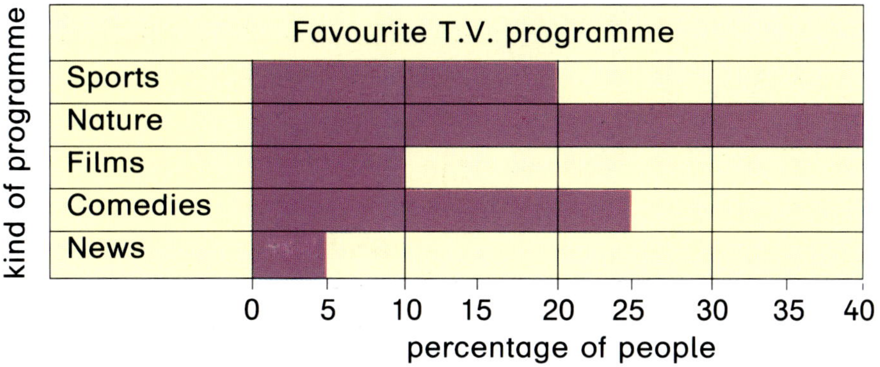

Remember:

$10\% = \frac{1}{10} = 0.1$

$20\% = \frac{2}{10} = 0.2$

and so on.

Answer these questions.

1. What percentage prefers news?
2. What fraction prefers nature?
3. What decimal prefers sports?
4. What fraction prefers comedies?
5. What decimal prefers films?

If 300 people were in the survey:

6. How many people preferred the news?
7. How many liked nature programmes?

If 500 people were in the survey:

8. How many people preferred sports programmes?
9. How many people preferred comedies?

If 1000 people were in the survey:

10. How many people preferred films?

Money and measures function machines

This function machine converts pence into pounds.

Use it to convert these amounts.

1. 999p **2.** 2545p **3.** 75p

4. 6312p **5.** 104p **6.** 1009p

Make a function machine to convert millilitres into litres.

Convert these amounts.

7. 1250 ml **8.** 35550 ml **9.** 750 ml

10. 4795 ml **11.** 920 ml **12.** 88375 ml

Make a function machine to convert metres into centimetres.

Convert these lengths.

13. 10.5 m **14.** 6.75 m **15.** 0.2 m

16. 25.05 m **17.** 0.8 m **18.** 13.95 m

Bills, bills and more bills

To use the telephone system costs £18.46 for 3 months

To rent a telephone costs £3.80 for 3 months

Each unit of a telephone call costs 4.2p

To work out a phone bill you add the system rental charge to the telephone rental charge. Then you multiply the number of units used by 4.2p and add it to the total.

Here is a bill for 6 months.

Mrs James	
System rental	18.46
System rental	18.46
Sub-total	36.92
Telephone rental	3.80
Telephone rental	3.80
Sub-total	7.60
196 units at 4.2p	8.23
Totals	36.92
	7.60
	8.23
Total bill	52.75

Make up bills for these people.

1. **Mrs Jones**

   3 months system and telephone rental charges.

   174 units used.

2. **Mr Smith**

   6 months system and telephone rental charges.

   265 units used.

3. **Miss Green**

   9 months system and telephone rental charges.

   562 units used.

4. **Ms Brown**

   1 year's system and telephone rental charges.

   983 units used.

Treasure map

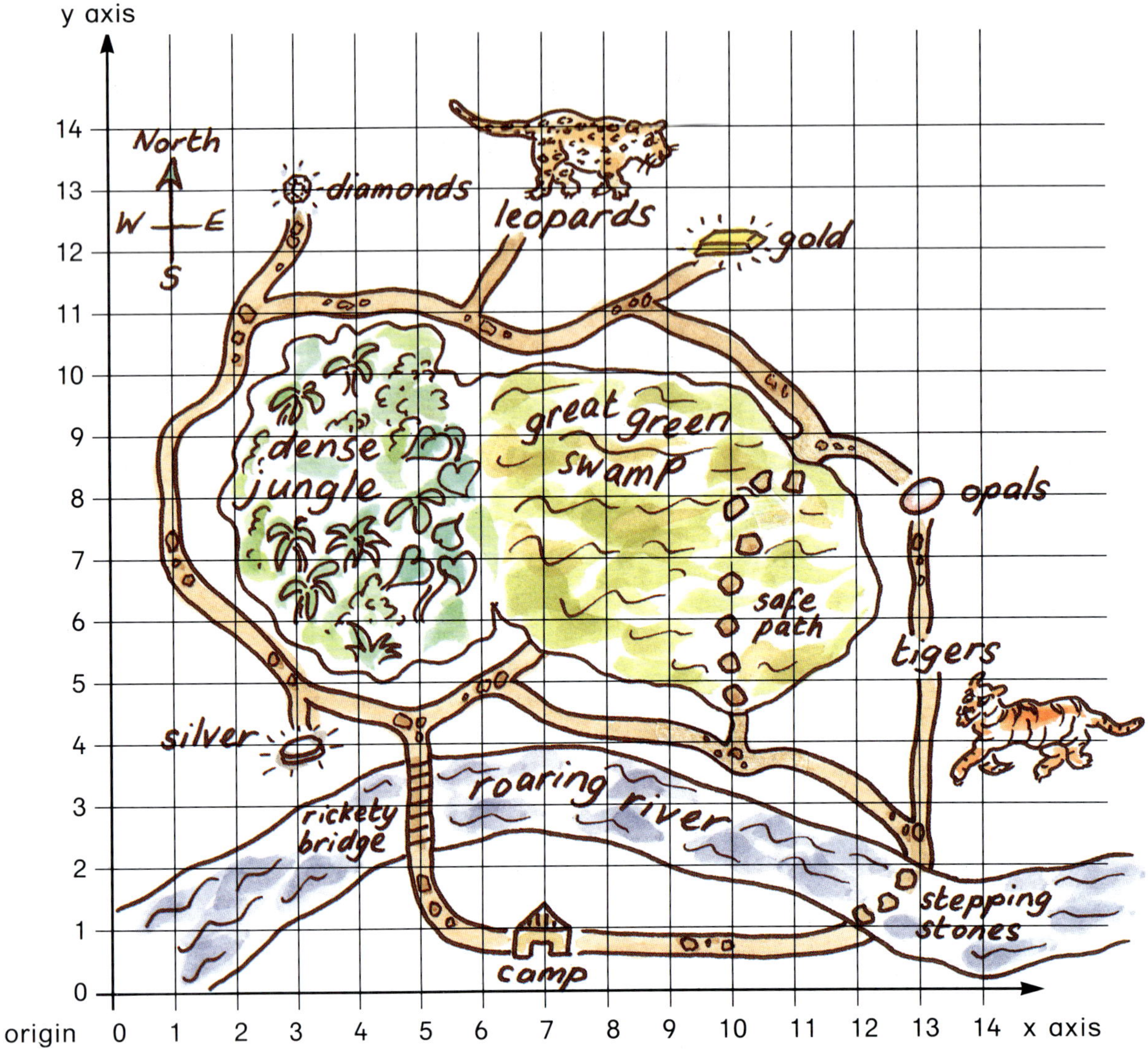

Use the map to answer these questions.

1. What would you find at (13,8)?
2. Write the ordered pairs for the location of the silver, the diamonds and the gold.

More questions on the next page ....

More map questions

3. Where does the safe path through the swamp start and finish?
4. If you went to (7,13) what danger would await you?
5. Write the ordered pairs to direct a friend from the camp to the opals. Use the stepping stones and avoid the tigers.
6. If you turned west at (10,8) where would you end up?
7. Use ordered pairs to describe the route from the diamonds back to the camp. You must use the path and the rickety bridge.
8. Find the shortest, safest route from the gold back to the camp. Write the ordered pairs for a friend to try.
9. Make your own map. Put in the co-ordinates. Make up some questions for a friend.

What am I?

Draw a grid with 12 points on the x axis and 9 points on the y axis.

Join the ordered pairs with lines.

START: (2,1) → (1,2) → (1,7) → (2,6) → (7,6)
(8,7) → (8,8) → (9,7) → (10,7) → (10,6)
(11,6) → (11,5) → (9,5) → (8,3) → (9,1)
(8,1) → (6,3) → (3,4) → (2,2) → (3,1) → (2,1) STOP

What have you drawn?

Measuring angles

Remember: to use a protractor for measuring angles place the centre of a protractor on the vertex of the angle.

Line up the base line of the protractor with one arm of the angle.

Start at 0 on the base line.

Read the number of degrees at the other arm.

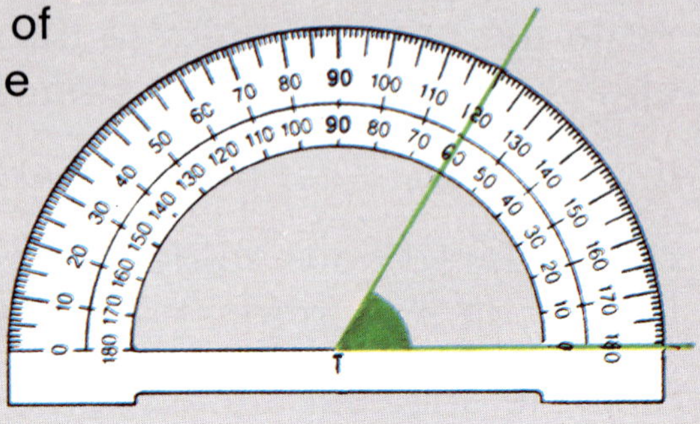

This angle measures 60°.

Use a protractor to measure all the angles in each of these shapes. Add up the angles in each shape. You may need to trace the shapes and extend the sides to measure the angles.

What do you notice?

1.

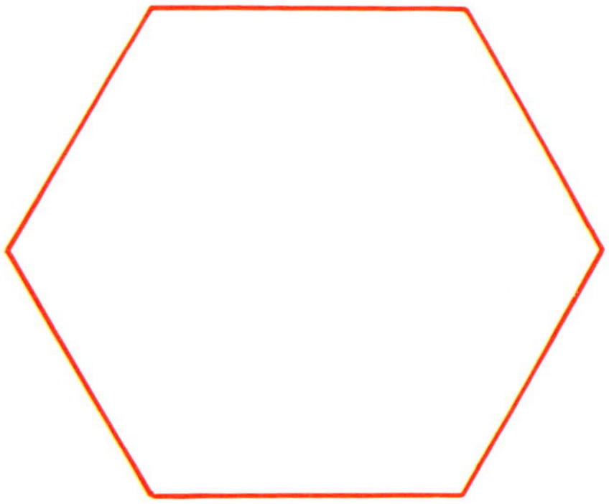

2.

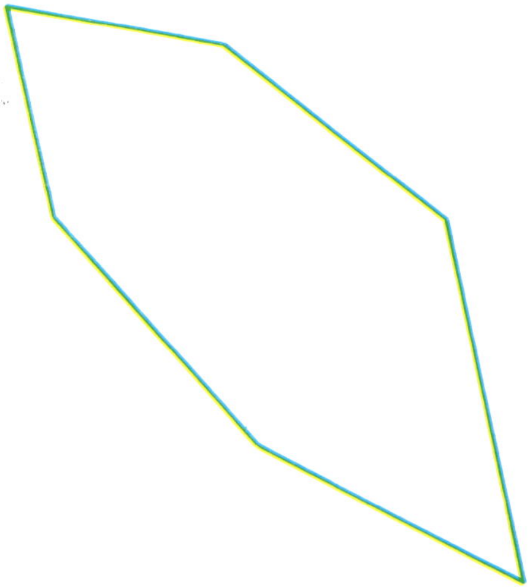

3.

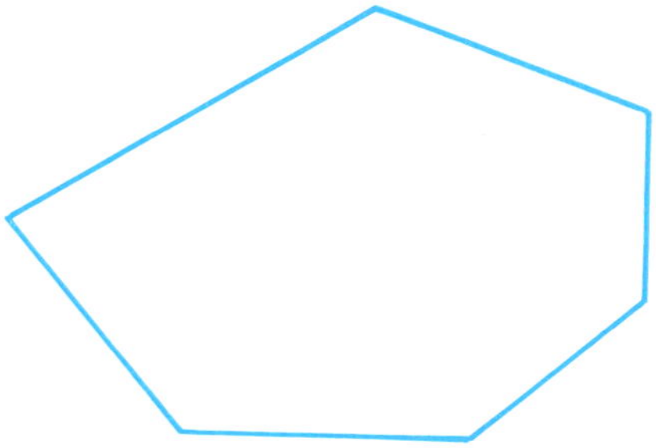

Drawing angles

You will need a protractor, a ruler and a pencil.

To draw an angle with a protractor, first draw the line you want.

Put the baseline of the protractor on your line.

Make sure that the centre of the baseline is exactly where you want the point of the angle to be.

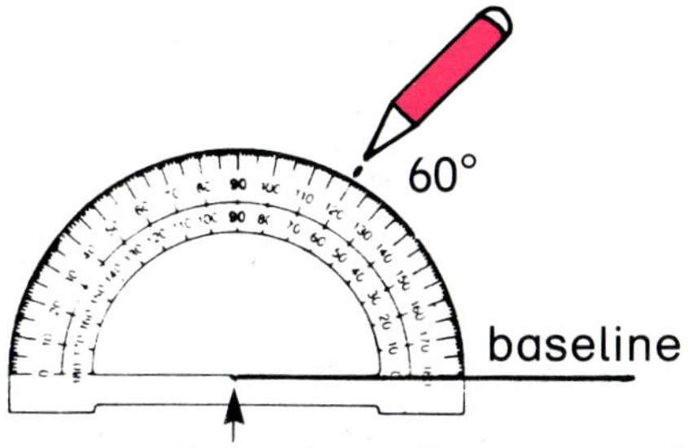

Follow the scale from the 0° **on your line** around the protractor to the angle you want. Make a mark.

Join the mark to the end of the line with a ruler.

Use a protractor and ruler to draw these angles.

1. 50°
2. 80°
3. 120°
4. 60°
5. 150°
6. 90°

Make the triangles

You will need a pair of compasses, a ruler, a protractor and a pencil.

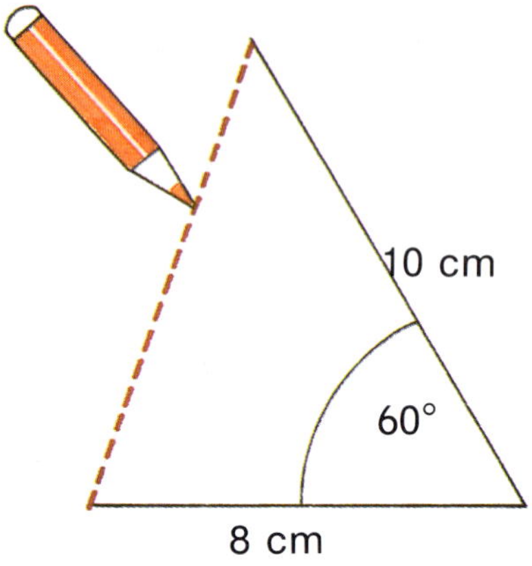

You can draw a triangle even if you do not know everything about it.

For example, if you know that two of the sides are 8 cm and 10 cm and their angle is 60°:

First draw the base (8 cm).

Use the protractor to measure an angle of 60°.

Draw another side along that angle, 10 cm long.

Finally, join up the two sides already drawn.

Measure these lines and angles. Draw them in your book.

Complete the triangles. Measure the third side.

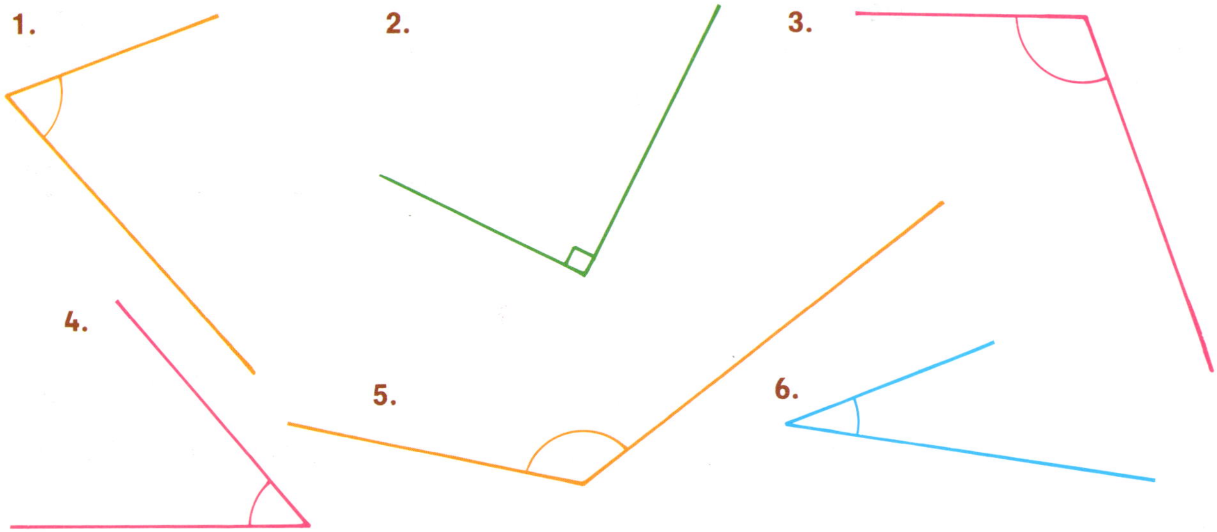

Two angles and the base

You can draw a triangle if you know the measurements of one side and two angles.

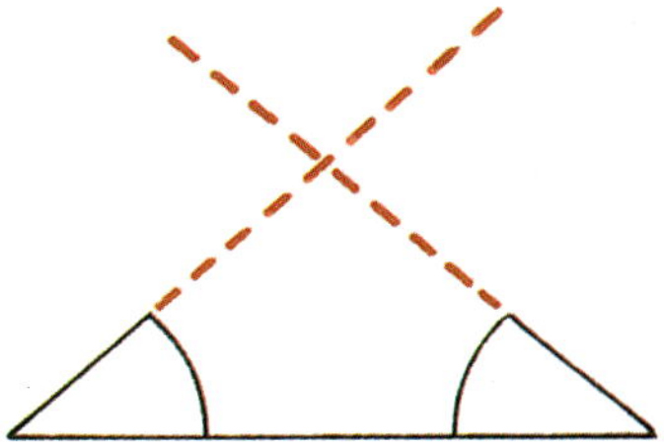

For example, 7 cm, 40°, 40°.

First draw the base (7 cm).

Use the protractor to measure and mark an angle of 40° at each end of the line.

Draw lines at 40° at each end of the base.

Where they cross is the other angle of the triangle.

Draw these triangles using this information.

1. base 10 cm
   angles 60°, 30°
2. base 5 cm
   angles 80°, 50°
3. base 6 cm
   angles 60°, 60°

If you know 3 sides

You will need compasses and a ruler.

If you know 3 sides of a triangle, for example, 8 cm, 7 cm, 5 cm, draw it like this.

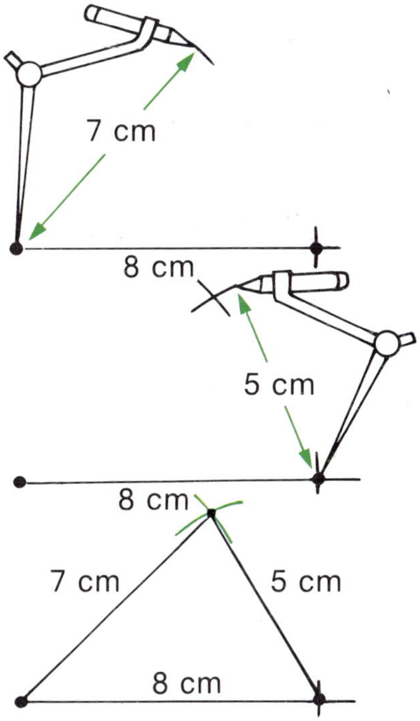

First, draw the base (8 cm). Next, set the compasses at 7 cm. Put the point on one end of the base and draw a large arc. Reset the compasses to 5 cm. Put the point on the other end of the base and draw another arc to cross the first arc. Use a ruler to join both ends of the base to the point where the arcs cross.

Draw these triangles.

4. 4 cm, 5 cm, 6 cm
5. 3 cm, 3 cm, 3 cm
6. 6 cm, 8 cm, 10 cm

Capacity and volume

This is a net of a cuboid.

When the cuboid is made it has a length of 2 cm, a breadth of 2 cm and a height of 1 cm.

Its volume is $2 \times 2 \times 1 = 4\ cm^3$.

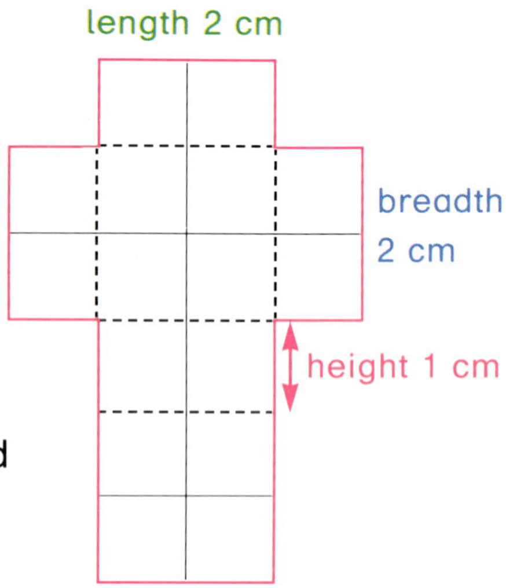

These nets can also be made into cubes and cuboids. Each square represents 1 square centimetre. Write their volumes.

1.

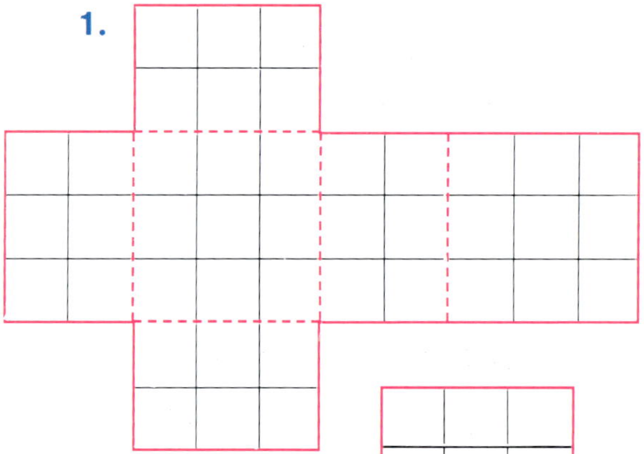

2.

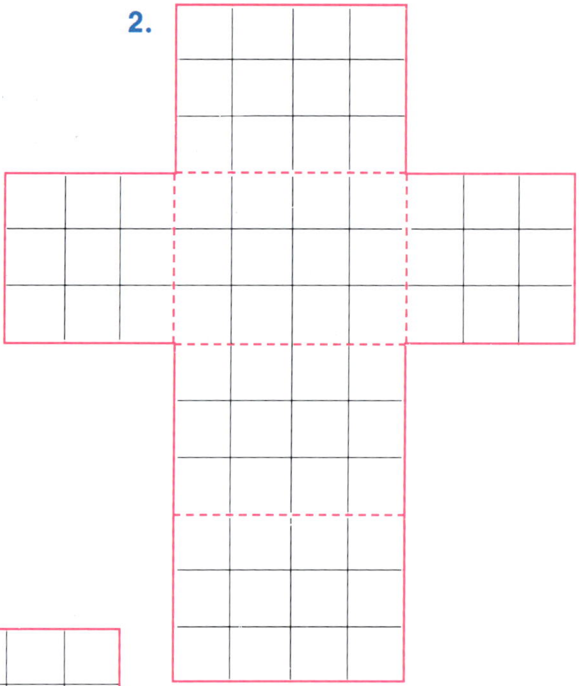

3.

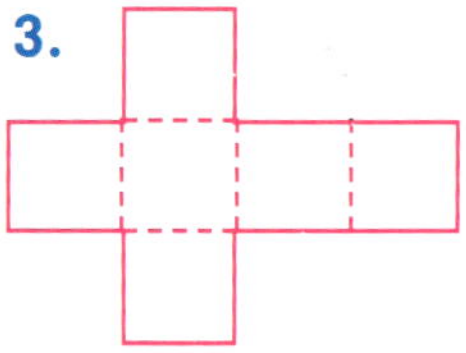

4.

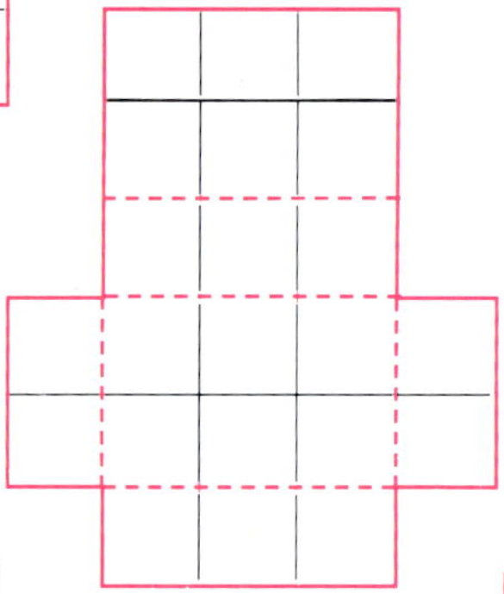

5.

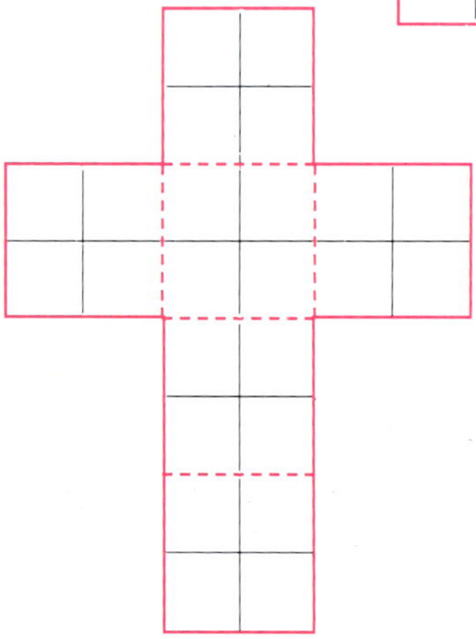

6.

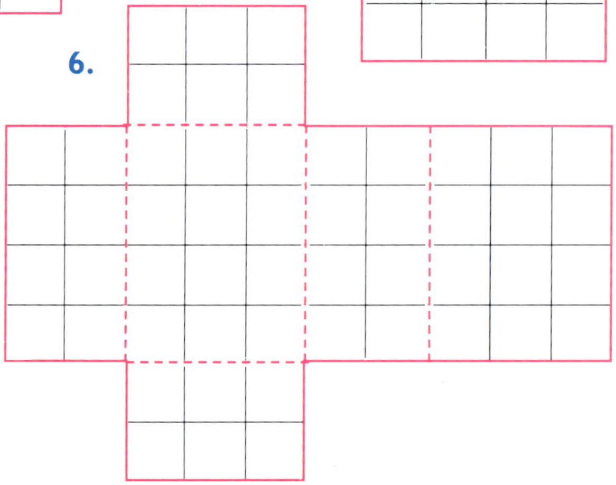

How much?

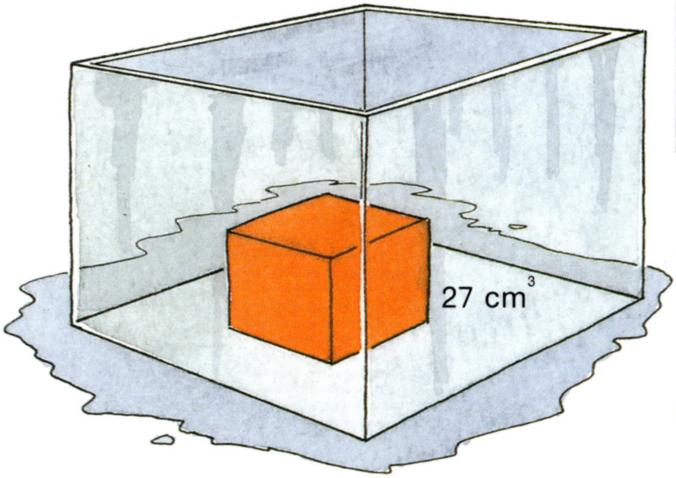

> Remember: 1 ml of water takes up 1 cm^3 of space and weighs 1 g.

This tank was filled with 500 ml of water.

A 3 cm x 3 cm x 3 cm cube was put into it.

Its volume of 27 cm^3 displaced 27 ml of water.

Displace means 'take the place of'.

27 ml of water overflowed.

How much water would these cubes and cuboids displace?

1. 10 cm x 6 cm x 2 cm
2. 13 cm x 8 cm x 4 cm
3. 11 cm x 16 cm x 2 cm
4. 9 cm x 3 cm x 3 cm
5. 12 cm x 5 cm x 4 cm
6. 14 cm x 6 cm x 5 cm

Find the volumes

You can find the volumes of all sorts of everyday objects.

Fill a displacement bucket with water. Place the object in it and use a measuring cylinder to measure the water which overflows.

Try these:

7. a brick
8. your hand
9. a pair of scissors

Fruit trees

Remember: a tree diagram uses the **same** question at each branch to sort items.

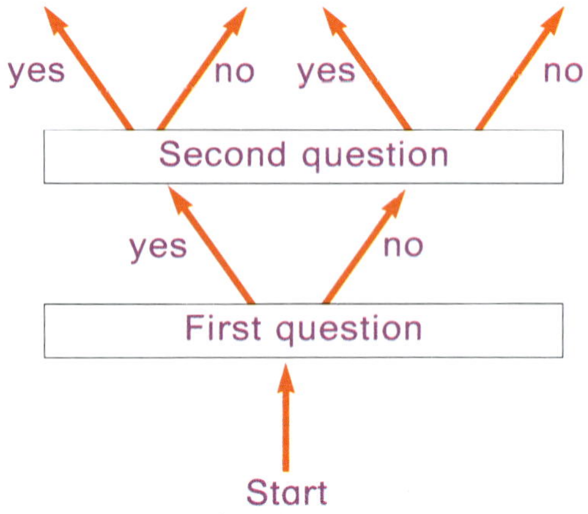

1. Draw a tree diagram to sort these fruits.
   Be careful when choosing questions for the yes/no branches.

Database of fruits

Name	colour	pips or stones	firmness
apple	red/green/yellow	pips	hard
strawberry	red	pips	soft
plum	red/yellow	stones	soft
peach	orange/yellow	stones	soft
orange	orange	pips	soft

Write the fruits which are sorted along these branches.

2. yes ⟶ yes branch
3. yes ⟶ no branch
4. no ⟶ yes branch
5. no ⟶ no branch

The solar system

Remember: a decision tree asks a **fresh** question at each branch to sort every item on to its own branch (see pages 66 and 67).

Use this database about the planets in the solar system to make a decision tree.

Name	Distance from the sun (millions of miles)	Diameter (miles)	Length of year (in Earth) time	Number of satellites	Atmosphere
Mercury	36	3010	88 days	0	none
Venus	67	7640	224 days	0	carbon dioxide
Earth	93	7926	365.25 days	1	nitrogen oxygen
Mars	141.5	4220	687 days	2	carbon dioxide
Jupiter	483.5	88730	11.8 years	12	hydrogen helium
Saturn	886.75	74130	29.5 years	10	hydrogen helium
Uranus	1783	29270	84 years	5	hydrogen helium methane
Neptune	2794	27840	164.8 years	2	hydrogen helium methane
Pluto	3661	3600	248.2 years	1	none

The kings and queens of England

Name	House	Accession	Died	Length of reign
Henry VIII	Tudor	1509	1547	38 yrs
Edward VI	Tudor	1547	1553	6 yrs
Mary	Tudor	1553	1558	5 yrs
Elizabeth I	Tudor	1558	1603	45 yrs
James I	Stuart	1603	1625	22 yrs
Charles I	Stuart	1625	1649	24 yrs
Charles II	Stuart	1660	1685	25 yrs
James II	Stuart	1685	1688	3 yrs
William III	Stuart	1688	1702	14 yrs
Anne	Stuart	1702	1714	12 yrs
George I	Hanover	1714	1727	7 yrs
George II	Hanover	1727	1760	33 yrs
George III	Hanover	1760	1820	60 yrs
George IV	Hanover	1820	1830	10 yrs
William IV	Hanover	1830	1837	7 yrs
Victoria	Hanover	1837	1901	64 yrs
Edward VII	Saxe-Coburg	1901	1910	9 yrs
George V	Windsor	1910	1936	26 yrs
Edward VIII	Windsor	1936	1936 (abdicated)	1 yr
George VI	Windsor	1936	1952	16 yrs
Elizabeth II	Windsor	1952	?	?

Showing information about kings and queens

The database on page 100 shows information about the kings and queens of England since 1509.

'House' shows the family name of the king or queen. For example, Henry VIII was Henry Tudor.

'Accession' is the year the king or queen came to the throne.

Choose the best type of graph to show the following information. You may need to draw a frequency table, choose a range and decide on a suitable scale. Draw the graph.

1. Which house had the most kings and queens and which the least?
2. What is the most common range of length of reign? For example, 1 to 10 years, 11 to 20 years, and so on.
3. How many kings and queens reigned in each century?
4. Make a chart or database showing information about something you are interested in. Draw graphs to show certain pieces of information to your friends.

Fair play

Here are some number cards.
If you pull out a number with a 5 in it you win!

1. How many chances of winning are there?
2. How many chances of losing are there?
3. Do you stand a good chance of winning?

4. Are these teams fair?

5. Is this a fair share?

6. How would you share these sweets fairly between two people?

7. Write down three things you think are unfair.
Write how you would make them fairer.

Fair and unfair spinners

These spinners were all made for games.

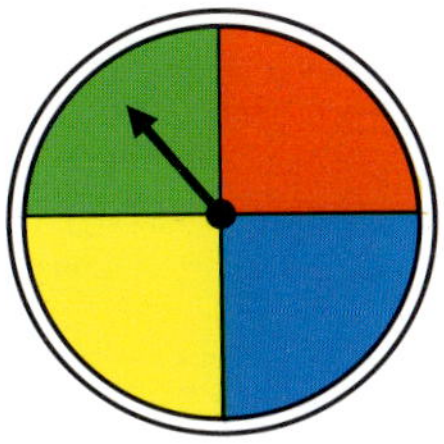

Anna's

Billy's

Colin's

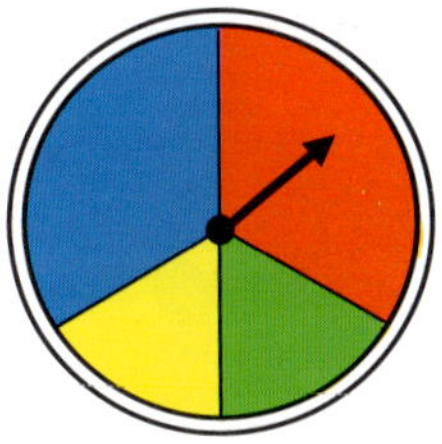

Debbie's

1. Whose spinners are unfair?
2. Whose spinners are fair?
3. Which colours could you get on Anna's spinner?
4. Which colours could you get on Colin's spinner?
5. Which colours on Debbie's spinner stand the best chance?
6. Which colours on Billy's spinner stand the worst chance?
7. Which fair spinner would you play with in a game with four colours?

Design your own spinner to have 6 colours.
Each colour must have a fair chance.

Design a spinner with the numbers 1, 2, 3 and 4.
Make the 3 have a better chance than the others.

Someone else's classroom

Their class and your class

1. How many children can you see in the classroom on page 104?
2. How many children are there in your class?
3. What is the difference?
4. On average, how many children are sitting at each group of tables in the picture?
5. How does this compare with your class?
6. Look at one group in the picture. What fraction of the group is one child? Then two children? What fraction of the group are you?
7. Look at the clock in the picture. What time does it show? What is the difference in hours and minutes from the time in your classroom?
8. Draw a sketch plan of the classroom in the picture.
9. Draw a sketch plan of your classroom. List the similarities or differences.
10. Design your ideal classroom. There may be some ideas in the picture that you like. For example, how the books are stored or the furniture arranged.

Glossary

acute angle An angle less than a right angle.

base The bottom side of a 2-D shape. The bottom face of a 3-D shape. In a prism it is an end face.

concentric circles Circles with the same centre.

co-ordinates Numbers used to show position on a chart or grid.

decision tree A diagram used for sorting by asking a series of questions with yes/no answers. Similar to a tree diagram.

digit 0, 1, 2, 3, 4, 5, 6, 7, 8, 9 are the digits. The numeral 546 is made from the digits 5, 4 and 6.

digital root The number obtained by adding all the digits of a number. The digital root of 25 is 7 (2 + 5).

factor A factor of a number is a number that will divide into that number exactly. 2, 3, 1 and 6 are all factors of 6.

function A combination of operations and numbers, for example, (x 3) or (x 5 ÷ 2)

horizontal A line parallel to the ground or, when represented on sheet of paper, parallel to the bottom and top edges.

hypotenuse The side opposite the right angle in a right-angled triangle.

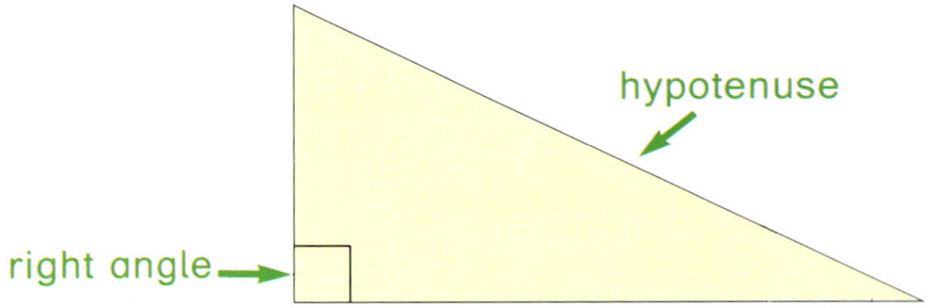

million A thousand thousand (1 000 000).

mixed number A quantity written as whole numbers and fractions. $1\frac{1}{4}$ and $3\frac{2}{3}$ are mixed numbers.

obtuse angle An angle more than one right angle but less than two right angles.

ordered pair A pair of co-ordinates which can be used for showing positions on a chart or grid. (6,2) is an ordered pair.

outcome The result; what happens.

parallel lines Straight lines that are always the same distance apart and never meet.

percentage (%) Out of a hundred. 15% means 15 out of 100.

perimeter The distance all the way round a shape.

perpendicular lines Lines at right angles to each other.

prism A 3-D shape with two congruent and parallel end faces.

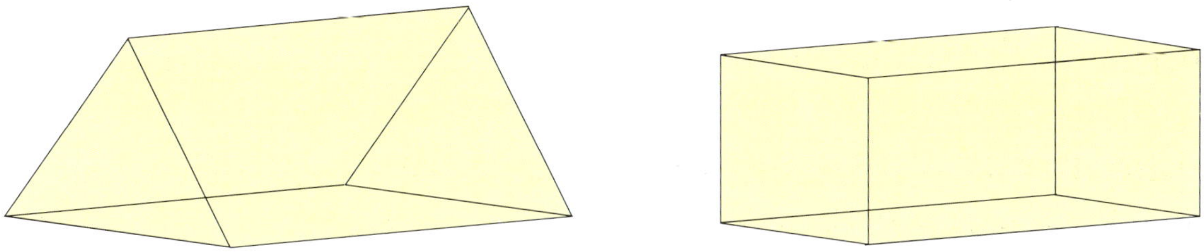

probability The likelihood of something happening.

product The result when numbers are multiplied.

pyramid A 3-D shape with a polygon as a base and whose other faces are triangles all meeting at a point.

reflex angle An angle that is more than two right angles.

regular polygon A polygon whose sides and angles are equal.

rotational symmetry A shape has rotational symmetry if it fits back into its 'frame' before it has made a full turn.

rounding Taking a number to the nearest whole number or the nearest ten, hundred, thousand, tenth, hundredth etc. 68 rounded to the nearest ten is 70.

stellated Made into a star shape, usually by adding a pyramid on to each face of a regular 3-D shape.

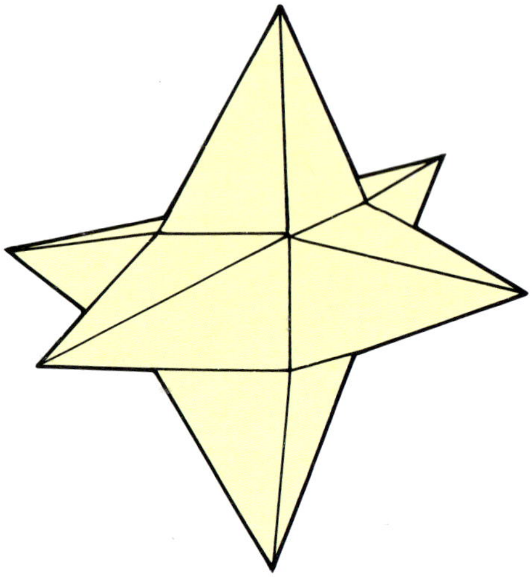

surface area The total area of all the faces of a 3-D shape.

tree-diagram A diagram on which items are sorted along different branches by asking questions with yes/no answers. Similar to a decision tree.

vedic square A multiplication square containing the digital roots of the products rather than the products themselves.

vertical A line perpendicular to the ground. When represented on paper, a line parallel to the sides of the paper.